OBJECT TECHNOLOGY IN APPLICATION DEVELOPMENT

DANIEL TKACH

Object Technology
IBM ITSO
San Jose, California

RICHARD PUTTICK

Systems Design Consultancy
IBM United Kingdon

The Benjamin/Cummings Publishing Company, Inc.
Redwood City, California • Menlo Park, California
Reading Massachusetts • New York • Don Mills, Ontario
Wokingham, U.K. • Amsterdam • Bonn • Sydney
Singapore • Tokyo • Madrid • San Juan

Executive Editor: Dan Joraanstad
Editorial Assistant: Melissa Standen
Production Editor: Teri Holden
Marketing Manager: Mary Tudor
Manufacturing Coordinator: Janet Weaver
Cover Design: Yvo Riezebos

Text Design: David Healy, First Image
Copyeditor: Nick Murray
Proofreader: Eleanor Renner Brown
Indexer: Mark Kmetzko
Composition and Illustrations: London Road Design

This document is intended to provide the customer with an introduction to the concepts, terminology, and practical issues related to the use of object technology in an application development environment.

It presents a perspective on how object technology is having an impact on the application development life cycle, the role of modeling and prototyping, the methodologies involved, the available languages and tools, the ongling standardization effors, and poroductivity metrics.

Library of Congress Cataloging-in-Publication Data

Tkach, Daniel
    Object technology in application development / Daniel Tkach,
  Richard Puttick.
      p.   cm.
    Includes bibliographical references (p.   ) and index.
    ISBN 0-8053-2572-7
    1. Object-oriented programming (Computer science) 2. Application
  software.   I. Puttick, Richard.   II. Title.
QA76.64.T56 1994   93-48035
005.1'1--dc20

ISBN 0-8053–2572–7
1 2 3 4 5 6 7 8 9 10-MA–98 97 96 95 94
The Benjamin/Cummings Publishing Company, Inc.
390 Bridge Parkway
Redwood City, CA 94065

Dedication

To the memory of my father, Abraham Tkach,
who taught me about writing books,
and to my mother, Frida Tkach,
who enjoys reading.

Daniel Tkach

To Bonk and Mickey.

Richard Puttick

Foreword

In the realm of production-quality software development, object technology has indeed proven its worth. For some application domains, time-to-market is the driving force. Here, we have witnessed the use of object-oriented methods and languages to bring projects such as a trading system to market in just a few months of development time. For other applications, such as for inventory management, resilience to change is the central force. Here, we have seen applications that have endured the ravages of wildly changing requirements, completed without having to throw schedules out the window.

Of course, just using an object-oriented method or language does not guarantee automatic success. As we would expect with any powerful technology, the object-oriented landscape is littered with the usual number of unsuccessful projects that usually failed to recognize the pragmatic issues of object technology.

This book, Object Technology in Applications Development, addresses such pragmatic issues, and is filled with important lessons that aid in delivering a successful application using object technology. Daniel Tkach and Richard Puttick, working at the IBM International Technical Support Center—San Jose, on worldwide transfer of object technology, have distilled much that will be useful to the object-oriented community from their own experience and their interactions with the IBM object technology research, development, and consulting groups.

—Grady Booch

Preface

"There is more to OOP than syntax!"
—Dr. Paul A. Luker

Object Technology and the Software Crisis

As computing power and user access facilities have increased with technological change, the complexity of the systems developed has also increased. More users are being served by computing systems and, aware of the available facilities, are becoming more demanding. User-friendly but complex graphical interfaces are becoming a standard requirement that is not easy to satisfy adequately with the current development tools and techniques. The maintenance backlog is also a severe burden that the MIS department has to cope with: most analysis, design, and documentation techniques used to implement today's applications do not accommodate changes.

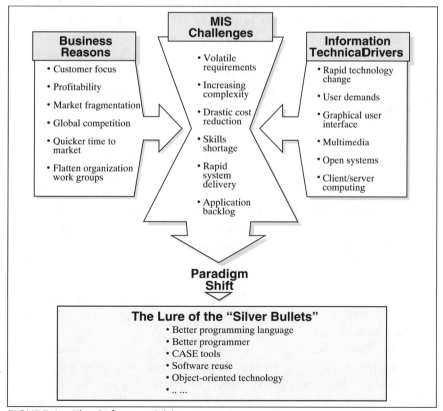

FIGURE 1   The Software Crisis

This situation, known as "the software crisis," calls for a solution that could boost the productivity of the MIS department by an order of magnitude, at least. It is doubtful that the change of just one element, be it the tool, the skill, the programming language or the paradigm, could produce such an increase in productivity. The attractiveness of such an instant solution was called by Fred Brooks "the lure of the silver bullet" [BR087]. But a sensible use of productive complementary tools and techniques, and a shift to a paradigm with proven advantages, may over time yield the desired results.

Object technology, which comprises object-oriented analysis (OOA), object-oriented design (OOD), and object oriented programming (OOP), represents a paradigm that has proven its productivity in a small team programming environment over the last 10 years. Now advances in OOA and OOD methodologies and in the languages and tools for OOP are providing an opportunity to achieve an equivalent increase in productivity in a corporate MIS environment. Although there is today no single "silver bullet that can by itself kill the monster of missed schedules, blown budgets, and flawed products that plague the application development projects" as Brooks so forcefully argued, the sound software principles of OOA and OOD, together with improvements in the languages, tools and training, and the establishment of a corporate reuse strategy, have the potential of materializing the needed productivity increase and the required cost reductions, while improving the credibility of the projects and plans of the organizations' MIS departments.

Audience

This book was written for people who plan to develop applications using object technology. We also hope to assist management in making decisions on modifying the application development environment to accommodate object orientation. Our overriding purpose has been to help our readers understand the role of object technology in the development of computer-based applications. To that end we discuss the impact that object technology can have on the application development life cycle, the role of modeling and prototyping, the methodologies involved, the available languages and tools, the ongoing standardization efforts, and the management issues that are key to successful application construction and delivery.

The main audience of this book is, therefore, the professional world of software development. However, our academic experience indicates that the real-world approach, distinctive of this book, will make it very useful to the senior and graduate university students of Software Engineering and Computer Science.

Contents

Chapter 1 provides an overview of object technology and introducts the terms most commonly used in this field. Chapter 2 looks at the application development environment. Chapter 3 covers the analysis and design phase activities in an object-oriented environment and categorizes the different approaches that the practitioners in the field advocate, while Chapter 4 takes up implementation issues. Chapter 5 addresses the complexities of building a user interface and the concepts and applications of visual programming tools.

Chapter 6 discusses the process of building an object-oriented application and the teamwork required, while Chapter 7 delves into the reuse constructs called frameworks, and their usefulness for productive application development. Chapter 8 reviews the requirements for persistent information in an object-oriented environment and the solutions provided by object databases. Chapter 9 analyzes the ongoing efforts to standardize the treatment of objects in order to facilitate compatibility across languages and platforms. Chapter 10 discusses the issues involved in managing and staffing object-oriented application development projects, and the structure and justification of a reuse organization. Finally, Chapter 11 provides a road map to application development, compatible with information modeling concepts.

Acknowledgments

This book is the result of the work done in the field of object technology at the IBM International Technical Support Center in San Jose, California. It includes the results of projects run at the Center, and sharing information and experiences with the IBM software laboratories of Santa Teresa, CA; Cary, NC; Rochester, MN; and Toronto, Canada. In addition, fruitful and stimulating exchanges have taken place with the IBM Object-Oriented Technology Center (OOTC), the IBM US Object-Oriented Consulting organization, and the IBM UK Know How Consultancy and Services Group. The projects at San Jose were staffed with specialists from IBM organizations of many countries, which contributed with their work and experience.

A first version of this book was published in 1992 by the same authors, as an IBM ITSO publication (known as a "redbook"). The present edition reflects the changes in the technology that have occurred since then and expands on many topics, providing a somewhat different perspective on many of them, as a result of practical experiences, and the maturing of viewpoints. It is impossible to name everyone who influenced our thinking, but we want to acknowledge the following people: Dr. Paul Luker of California State University, Chico, for his detailed and precise comments that contributed to enhance the book's contents; Walter Fang of IBM Canada for his ideas and drawings; Peter Demetrios, formerly of the IBM Cary Lab, presented the developer's viewpoint; Ghica van Emde Boas-Lubsen of IBM Netherlands built the tool used for the documentation and participated in an early version of the sample application. Meaningful discussions were held, among others, with Dave Collins (IBM Research), Lou Thomason (IBM Open Architecture), Bob Quinn (IBM Santa Teresa Lab), Chamond Liu (Skill Dynamics), Alistair Cockburn (IBM Consulting), Guillermo Lois (OOTC), Andy So (IBM Hong Kong), Tom Donahoe (IBM San Diego), Alessandro Mottadelli (IBM Italy), and many other specialists whose contribution we want to acknowledge. Dave Thomas, of IOTI, Canada, supported and encouraged this endeavor.

This work would not have been possible to accomplish without the active support of Brett Paskin, ITSC San Jose AD Manager. Brian Winborn, ITSC San Jose Center manager, and Norm Zimmerman, ITSO director, provided an environment of empowerment that allowed new ideas to blossom and bear fruit.

Thanks are due to our editors, Maggie Cutler and Shelly Langman. Special thanks are due to the Benjamin/Cummings staff members Dan Joraanstad and Teri Holden, for their support and understanding.

D.S.T.
R.A.P.

Contents

Introduction to Application Development

In this chapter we provide an overview of the application development process and introduce the terms and concepts most commonly used in this field, emphasizing their application to real-world modeling.[1]

1.1 The Role of Modeling in Software Development

The development of software applications faces quality and productivity problems that arise from the interpretation of business requirements as described by prospective users. As development proceeds from the requirements phase to application delivery in the application development life cycle, this description often loses its fidelity and timeliness in the wake of the increasingly complex characteristics of the proposed systems and applications. In addition, there is the difficulty of implementing and managing changes, which must be understood, developed, and integrated into existing systems in a reasonable time frame.

---

1. *A more detailed explanation of the concepts related to object technology is provided in Chapter 2, "Object Technology Concepts."*

A model of a system can help us to understand and communicate requirements. A model is a representation of a system. Models can explicitly represent both the structure and the functional behavior of a system. Users can analyze model diagrams and make qualitative guesses about the attributes and behavior of the actual system that they represent. Object technologies are basically modeling technologies. The models built describe entities called **objects** and the relations among them. These entities are defined in the analysis phase, which is also called the *real-world modeling* phase, and represent business objects, that is, objects of the real world of the business application.

Model objects include packages of data that describe the attributes of the object. Those attributes are associated with procedures specific to each object that are called *access methods*, or simply **methods**, and describe the behavior of the objects. The important consideration here is that the object data should (or, depending on the implementation language, must) be accessed only through those methods. Allowing access to the data only through the object's methods is called **encapsulation**, which contributes to enforcing a correct use of the data, because the meaning, or *semantics*, of the data is defined by the operations on that data. The way to invoke these methods is to produce an event, usually by sending a **message** to an object that asks it to carry out one of its methods. The message includes the object's name and the method whose execution is required. If additional data is needed, it can be passed on in the message as **arguments.**

An important step in building an object model is to classify the objects, that is, to determine categories of objects that make sense within the context of the application. For instance, if the objects to be considered are a pair of pliers, a wrench, and a screwdriver, it probably makes sense to classify them as "tools." This classification is a process of abstraction, where the describing concept (tools in this case) is called a **class,** which is a description that covers the most important attributes of a given application. In object technology, a model is usually built using classes, not with representations of the real-world objects: these are called *class instances.*

Objects and classes can be related to other objects and classes, respectively. The relationships are usually called **associations** when applied to classes, and sometimes **links** when applied to objects. For instance, a class Person can be associated with the class Tools by the relationship Uses. At the instance level, each person could be using one or more tools, and a tool can be used by one or more persons. This "one-or-more" consideration is called the *multiplicity* of the association.

The concept of abstraction can be carried even further, so it is possible to define classes that are the abstraction of the common features of existing classes. Supermarket aisle denominations (Baby Needs, Canned Foods) provide good examples of abstraction, as do the titles of classified advertising sections in the newspapers (Furniture, Services). The common characteristics of high-level classes can be "inherited" by the less general classes without the need of repetition: this is called ***inheritance.***

This model-building strategy has some important advantages [TAY91]. All the higher-level classes, as well as the model itself, are general-purpose in nature and can be reused in future projects. This is good-quality code, developed and tested thoroughly for one application. When code is used again in other applications, part of the development effort is already done, and the quality of the reused code contributes to the quality of the new application. The existence of reusable components of code also facilitates the rapid building of a basic working version of the application, called a *prototype,* that can be used for proof-of-concept and as a checkpoint for the correct interpretation of the user requirements.

The core of an object is a data structure. Data-structure-centered models are more stable foundations for application development than function-centered models, because the requirements for change are more frequent at the function level than at the data level. In addition, solutions based on high-level models are flexible, because it is possible to implement different specific solutions at a lower level without changing the higher-level classes.

MIS shops can therefore respond to the requirements for better and faster software construction by using object technology. The process starts with the building of the first applications and the abstraction and collection of libraries of reusable classes. These classes can be used to construct other models of applications, whose quality can be tested through rapid prototyping. The result of each development stage feeds back to the earlier stages, thereby enhancing the model with new relationships and classes.

In an application development environment, such as the one defined by the IBM AD/Cycle framework, classes are cataloged in a repository according to the specifications of an information model. The repository can be used throughout the application development life cycle, supporting all phases of the model-driven development. It is expected that object-oriented upper-CASE tools will populate the repository. Developers should be able to use generator, language, and knowledge-based system (KBS) tools to extract the classes from the repository and use them to build business applications.

1.2 Toward the Software Factory: Construction from Parts

A major theme of object technology is ***construction from parts***, that is, the fabrication, customization, and assembly of component parts into working applications. These parts (objects, classes, or sets of classes and relationships) are modular application components, with well-defined interfaces and methods encapsulating data structures. They may come from a variety of sources (including languages, generators, KBS, and object-oriented tools). The parts may be built in-house, but they could also be purchased from specialized object-oriented software vendors.

Reusable parts may be involved in several levels of the development process. At the language level, there are class libraries, which are the basic constructs provided with object-oriented languages. At the system level, classes are organized in frameworks supporting, for instance, database access or client/server computing. At the industry or business level, there may be class libraries along with a general model that serves as a template (framework) for a specific industry-oriented set of applications (such as generic inventory or banking systems). At the enterprise level, class libraries together with an enterprise model can reflect the specific characteristics and requirements of the enterprise.

Object technology is a productive extension of the tools and techniques used until now in the application development environment. This technology has been introduced across the development cycle. Currently available languages, generators, database management systems, tools, and methodologies support object orientation as a valid alternative for enterprises that are looking for solutions to their software crises.

1.3 The Application Development Environment

Our description of an application development environment will be based on the schema proposed by IBM for AD/Cycle. AD/Cycle is application development framework defined by IBM originally for Systems Application Architecture (SAA™) environments, but later extended to a full, open, distributed environment. It was designed as an evolutionary framework, a long-term strategy that organizes and integrates application development objectives. The AD/Cycle framework describes a model of the complete application development life cycle. It consists of five phases, as shown in Figure 1.1. The five blocks toward the top of the diagram show the normal phases of the development of an application:

1. Requirements

2. Analysis/Design

3. Implement/Produce

4. Building/Testing

5. Production/Maintenance

The bar across the top represents the cross-life-cycle tools. These are the tools and services that span all development life cycle functions. They include process and project management, documentation, and reuse. The bar across the bottom is the application development platform (ADP), the means of integration and the storage area for all information pertaining to the enterprise, its development processes, application data, and the applications themselves. The ADP components include workstation services, library services, repository services, and the AD/Cycle Information Model. The six blocks in the center of the diagram illustrate how tools are grouped by use within the individual life-cycle phases.

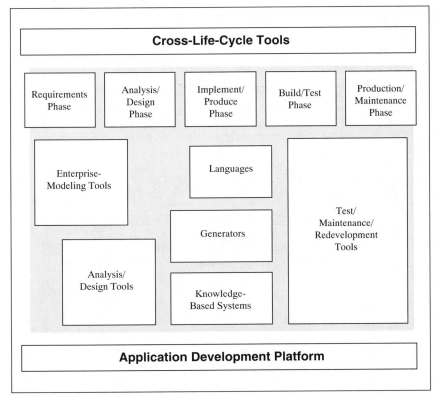

FIGURE 1.1   The AD/Cycle framework

Requirements

The objective of the requirements phase is to provide a statement, expressed in business terms, that defines and describes the problem domain (Figure 1.2). The requirements phase involves the process of modeling a business enterprise to describe its present and future business structure and functions. AD/Cycle supports enterprise-modeling tools and the storing of business models in a repository, not necessarily centralized. The classical structured enterprise models represent the enterprise as viewed by executive and senior management. Advanced modeling techniques can enhance these rather static descriptions by adding capabilities for performing dynamic enterprise simulation.

A planning stage precedes the actual modeling and provides input to the modeling activity. This input may be represented in charts and models. During structured enterprise modeling, the charts and models are expanded to give a complete definition of the problem domain. This provides a context for further technical analysis and design work. The tools used in structured enterprise modeling produce a variety of outputs, such as functional and process decomposition diagrams, logical data models, usage and responsibility matrices, and property descriptions.

Each business function in the functional decomposition diagram is expanded into the actual business processes that make up that function. The decomposition then continues by subdividing each business

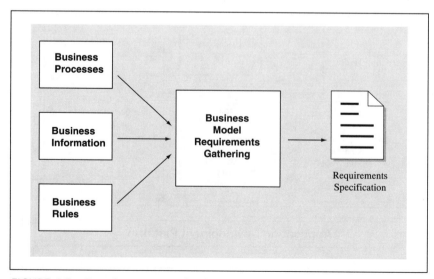

FIGURE 1.2   Requirements gathering

process into its constituent processes. This subdivision continues until it reaches the stage of defining a business process in terms of imperative statements that describe, step by step, how an application program would perform a specific business task. This is the lowest level at which a business process can be meaningfully defined. Process decomposition diagrams usually have exactly the same format as the functional decomposition diagrams upon which they are based.

In a similar way, the conceptual information model is transformed into a logical data model that defines the data needs of the problem domain. A logical data model depicts the detailed view or views of the data that an application will require.

The logical data model at this stage is often *normalized*. Normalization is a formal process that groups related facts into common entities and removes duplicate definitions from the model. Normalized data models from various problem domains can be compared in order to identify and reconcile areas of intersection.

Usage and responsibility matrices are constructed to show the relationships among processes, entities, business goals, critical success factors, and other output from the planning stage. Property descriptions contain detailed information about processes, entities, and other output from the planning stage. These are normally represented in tabular format for ease of reference in the later design stages. Requirements gathering thus produces a record of the business in terms of processes, information (data), and business rules.

Analysis and Design

Analysis

The analysis phase analyzes the business requirements (Figure 1.3). The result of this phase depends on the modeling approach. The result of classical structural analysis, for instance, can be described by diagrams that represent models of different aspects of the business applications, such as entity-relationship (E-R), decomposition, relational database, and data flow diagrams.

The importance of each type of model has shifted with the evolution of the technology. In the 1970s, the original form of structured analysis emphasized the modeling of functions in a system, using the data flow diagram as the main graphical modeling tool. Structural analysis incorporated the data component but did not give it proper emphasis. Not until the mid 1980s did the more "modern" forms of structured analysis appear, incorporating the E-R diagram for data

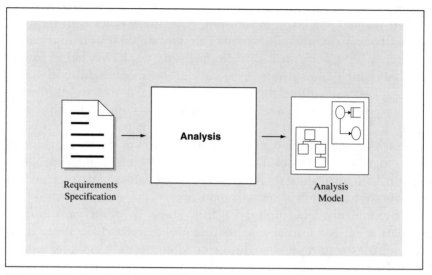

FIGURE 1.3   Application analysis

modeling and the state-transition diagram for real-time systems. The most modern variants of structured analysis and design shift the perspective of systems analysis noticeably toward the user [YOU92].

Object-oriented analysis is derived from the data-model-centered approach. Objects in the object model correspond to objects in the real (business) world. In addition to the state of the variables of the object data structure, however, objects have a behavioral component, defined by the set of procedures (methods) that allow access to data and interaction with other objects. Some variants of object modeling emphasize the data and state-related aspects [SHL88], [SHL91], [RUM91]; others emphasize the behavioral aspects [GIB90], [WIR89], [WIR90].

Design

The design phase in AD/Cycle focuses on defining the software to implement the application (Figure 1.4). The objective of this phase is to specify the computer-related aspects of the application such as screen designs, report designs, logical and physical database structures, data views for application programs, pseudocode or minispecifications for program modules, subsystems definitions, and, in the case of distributed applications, networking considerations [MON91]. Prototyping or simulation techniques can then be used to refine these aspects in collaboration with the user or expert.[2]

---

2. There is a difference between prototyping and simulation. In a prototype, the intention is to provide proof of the original concept and produce the final production code in an iterative fashion, based on the prototype's structure and sometimes on its code. In a simulation, the intention is to prove the design intent by producing a replica of the system, using specialized disposable code, and then use the experience gained in that process to build a production system, using more robust programming techniques.

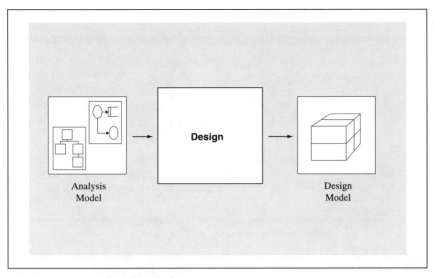

FIGURE   1.4 Application design

Database Design   The design of physical databases can proceed in parallel with application design. The information gathered during the requirements phase is used to define the contents of the database. In the analysis phase, this information is expanded.

In the design phase logistic details are added. This information will include the expected volumes of each type of entity, the projected update frequency and rate, the expected number of accesses over a given time period, and other relevant usage statistics. Such information is especially critical to the design of distributed database systems.

External Design Specifications   Up to this point in AD/Cycle, the emphasis has been on meeting the business requirements of the application. The business-related characteristics derived during the analysis phase do not take into account technical considerations and constraints related to the implementation.

The production of an *external design specification* at the end of the analysis and design phase is sometimes used to distinguish the business domain from the solution domain, although this document may not be a practical working paper when an iterative development methodology is chosen. Often, however, the various business groups who will eventually use the application are the target audience for the external design specification, because they must formally approve it before authorizing any further investment in application development.

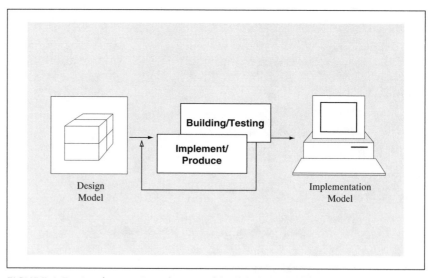

FIGURE 1.5   Implement/produce and building/testing

Implement/Produce

The implement/produce phase emphasizes implementation and coding. The output from the analysis and design phase must be transformed into the input required to build an industrial-strength application (Figure 1.5).

Developers must consider environmental details, such as security requirements and recovery strategies, and produce final documentation standards, testing schedules, and scripts. They must also decide which parts of the application are to have code automatically generated, which are to be implemented in a KBS, which must be manually programmed, and which can reuse prototype code generated during the design phase.

Code Generators   Many of the tool sets used in support of the requirements and the analysis and design phases can automatically generate application code. The code generated is usually based on a transactional paradigm, which uses a transaction manager to provide communications support. A few of the more sophisticated tool sets produce client/server computing applications.

Knowledge Processing   Knowledge-processing programs are those whose competence at a task derives from knowledge about the task domain. This knowledge can be represented using several paradigms, such as production rules (IF-THEN rules), frames (prototypical descriptions of objects), and first-order logic. The tools used to represent that knowledge include *expert tools* and languages. Expert tools provide facilities to store knowledge, and they employ inference modules for problem solving based on the stored knowledge. Fifth-generation languages, such as Prolog, structure knowledge in the form of database entries and logic predicates and perform deductions by theorem-proving.

Languages   Languages include the traditional third-generation languages, such as COBOL, C, and PL/I. Other AD/Cycle languages, such as Smalltalk/V PM™, used for building object-oriented applications, can also be considered as graphical user interface (GUI) generators.

Building and Testing

The building and testing phase is concerned with the integration of the new function into the existing application set. The actual activities performed during this phase depend on the characteristics of the application's operating environment and the procedures defined for each installation. Tools such as the IBM Workstation Interactive Test Tool (WITT) can be used for developing test cases, capturing test-case information, and reporting the results of testing.

Production and Maintenance

The production and maintenance phase represents the working life of the application. When an application goes into real-life production, provisions have to be made to integrate it with the rest of the application, as well as for running in parallel during the first period with the old applications, cutover considerations, and so on.

From then on, and during the lifetime of the application, it is reasonable to expect that changes will be required to accommodate business changes, add enhancement, or fix problems. These changes and fixes are referred to as the *maintenance* of the application. This activity is supported through a number of mechanisms, including

- Redevelopment tools and techniques

- Impact-analysis tools

- Build, release, and control facilities

1.4 Development Approaches

All of the major application development approaches include the five AD/Cycle development phases. The approaches differ in the disciplines and controls that are used to manage the development process and in the emphasis placed on each phase. Three of the most common

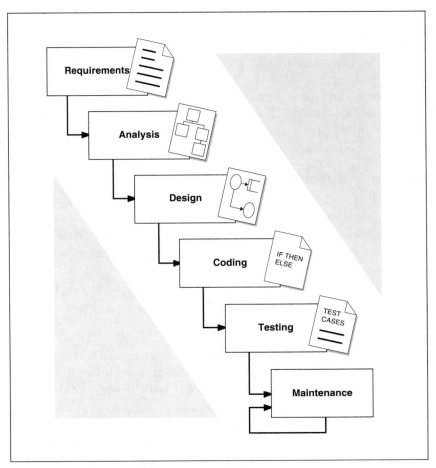

FIGURE 1.6   The waterfall process model

are the waterfall approach, the spiral approach, and the incremental approach.

The Waterfall Approach

Waterfall is the name given to the traditional approach to application development (Figure 1.6). It is characterized by requiring a formal sign-off for each phase before work commences on the next phase. Once a phase is completed, it is not usually revisited. The development phases used in the waterfall approach are

1. Requirements definition

2. Analysis and design

3. Solution production

4. Building and testing

5. Production and maintenance

The waterfall approach may be adequate when there is a complete understanding of user requirements, and the analysis and design are performed by highly skilled people. However, many problems may result from the inflexibility of this approach. For instance, when the user first sees the system running, it is usually in the last stage of development. If the user does not like the result, or if there are changes in the requirements, a major revision would be required in order to accommodate any modifications.

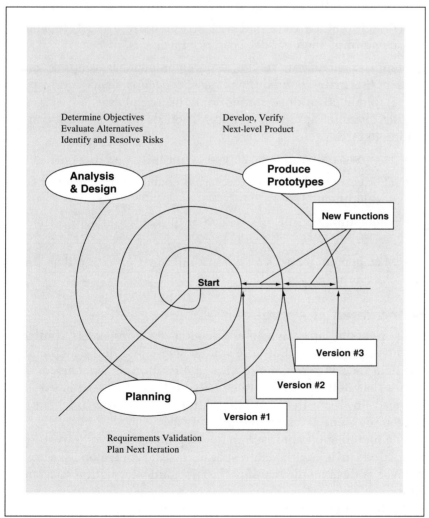

FIGURE 1.7   The spiral process model

The Spiral Approach

The spiral approach is based on building several levels of prototypes and performing a risk analysis at each level (Figure 1.7). The five development phases are still followed, but the emphasis placed on each phase differs. The steps are

1. Planning for the initial or next iteration of the problem solution

2. Determining the objectives, alternatives, and constraints

3. Performing a risk analysis

4. Producing a prototype solution

5. Validating the prototype against the current objectives

6. Performing the whole process again until a product, capable of being implemented, has been produced.

Step 1 is analogous to the requirements phase, steps 2 and 3 represent the analysis and design phase, and steps 4 and 5 correspond to the implement/produce and building/testing phases.

This dynamic approach to application development is good for medium to large projects, where

- The total problem to be solved is not fully understood.

- The real world can be expected to change during the period of development.

- The solution itself might have an unknown effect on the real world.

- Management focus is on quality and function rather than financial controls.

The Incremental Approach

The incremental approach to application development is similar to the waterfall approach. Both use similar stages, but in the incremental approach the development of the application is conceived as a process that delivers first a reduced set of functions which is then enhanced in each iteration. In addition, there can be iterations between the steps as indicated in Figure 1.8.

The incremental approach to development starts to deliver limited function earlier, with a corresponding faster return on investment. However, it does require careful planning and very tight management control.

All three development approaches are valid and can be used for building object-oriented applications. However, since one of the advantages

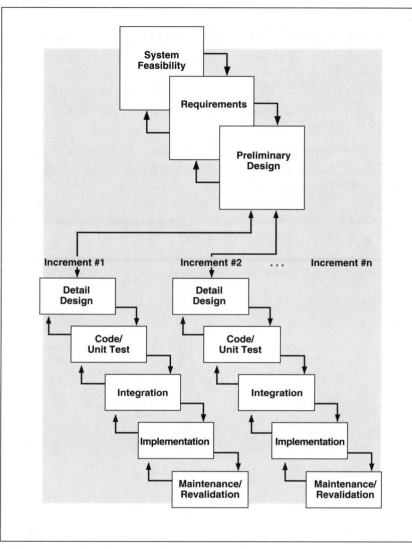

FIGURE 1.8   The incremental process model

of object technology is the ability to rapidly build a model and perform early prototyping, approaches that allow feedback and incremental development are better for object-oriented application development than the basic waterfall approach.

1.5 Summary

- The development of an application goes through five process phases: requirements, analysis, design, implementation, testing, and production.

- There are several process models that can be used in the application development life cycle. They include the waterfall, spiral, and incremental models.

- All development approaches can be used for building object oriented applications. However, since one of the advantages provided by object technology is the ability to rapidly build a model and perform early prototyping, feedback-enabling approaches are more adequate for object-oriented application development than the basic waterfall approach.

2

Object Technology Concepts

In this chapter we introduce the terminology and main concepts involved in object technology and analyze the benefits of using the technology. Object technology is a specific way of structuring applications. To apply this technology successfully in software development, however, we must adopt new ways of thinking about programs.

Application development is significantly more complex today than it was a decade ago. Interactive GUIs, distributed or cooperative processing, very large integrated applications and databases, heterogeneous environments, and rapid changes in business units have increased the application backlog, even though new software engineering methods were expected to reduce that backlog.

Object technology is seen as an important step toward the industrialization of software that can help to transform programming from an arcane craft to a systematic manufacturing process [TAY91]. Object orientation holds out the promise of increasing productivity in software development and improving the quality of software. At the same time it should help to relate computer systems more closely to the real world.

2.1   What Is an Object?

In daily life, objects are usually understood to be things of the real world, such as tables, chairs, and order forms. Objects have properties; for instance, a table has legs, is made of a certain wood, and has a location. The values of these properties together define the **state** of the object. For example, a table may have four legs, be made of beechwood, and be located in room A09. It is possible to perform actions on objects: a table can be created or destroyed, and its location changed.

Similar objects can be grouped into a *class.* The beechwood table is an *instance* of the class Table. Sometimes a class describes a more generic concept. The beechwood table is a table, but also a piece of furniture, like the chair at its side. One can say that Furniture is a *superclass* of both the class Table and the class Chair. All chairs and tables also have all properties defined for furniture: both the beechwood table and the chair by its side inherit the properties of having a color, a weight, legs, and a location.

Tables are relatively simple, passive objects. More complicated objects, such as a washing machine, consist of many parts, which are objects themselves. A washing machine can perform a sequence of washing steps, some of them in parallel. When all steps are completed, it may beep to signal that it has finished.

2.2   Computer Representation

In a computer application there are no objects in the sense described above. The computer contains an electronic representation of an abstract model that represents some parts of the real world. Before the advent of object technology, compilers for coding languages such as Assembler, COBOL, and PL/I were used to translate processes and data structures to the representation used by the computer. The human exchange of information about these processes was facilitated by the use of data flow diagrams, decision tables, abstract data types, and other descriptive conventions that allowed the programmer to state the problem at a higher level than the code. Several types of tools, such as CASE tools, were developed to perform different levels of translations, such as the translations from the real world to data flow diagrams, from data flow diagrams to decision tables, and from decision tables to a programming language such as COBOL.

The use of very different representations, even with the help of computer-based tools in the translation process, had an unwanted side effect: end users, analysts, designers, and programmers talked in very different languages. Because the various translation steps were not seamless, sometimes the resulting application was not quite what the end user had in mind.

Object technology represents an effort to overcome this problem. One goal of the technology is that end users, analysts, and programmers should be able to talk about the same things: the objects of the application. An implicit requirement, therefore, is that the objects should represent elements of the user's real world. For example, for an ordering system, end users may talk about order forms, customers, and products. They will define the properties of these objects and the actions that can be performed on the properties, such as the change of address of a customer. In an object-oriented approach, the analyst will define a model using the same terms as the end user to describe entities with the properties and behavior the end user is talking about, and will build a model that describes relations among these entities. Based on this model, the programmer will produce a program organized in such a way that the data (which are the properties of the objects), and the *methods* (which are the operations that can be performed on the data) stay together (at least conceptually), and the only way to access the data is through these methods (Figure 2.1).

This grouping of data with its access methods is called an object. Thus, object-oriented programming is the implementation of entities that represent objects in the real world in a computer environment.

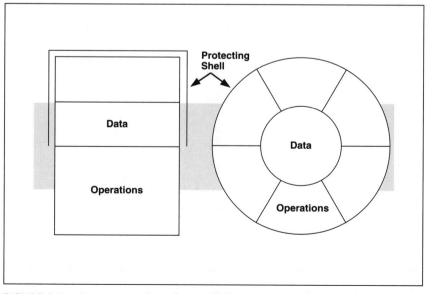

FIGURE 2.1   Representations for an object

2.3 **Object-Oriented Concepts and Terminology**

Any new technology fosters the creation of a new terminology, or jargon, to describe the concepts it handles. This terminology allows for greater precision when referring to aspects of the technology, and more efficient communication among practitioners of the discipline.

Object technology, which is also sometimes referred to as *object orientation,* has its own terminology. Since object orientation started with the creation of object-oriented programming languages (OOPLs), there are some differences in the terminology used with different languages. This book uses the terminology derived from the OOPL Smalltalk. Authors with a background in other OOPLs, such as C++, Eiffel, or CLOS, may use some different terms, or use the same terms with slightly different connotations. Still, most practitioners agree that, for any programming language or methodology to be called *object-oriented,* it must support the concepts of *objects, classes*, and *inheritance.*

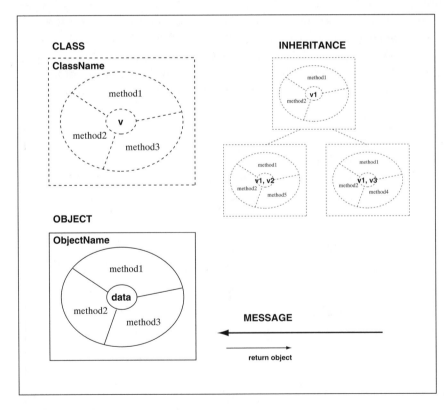

FIGURE 2.2   Object-oriented concepts

The definitions of object-oriented concepts listed below are based on the publications [WEG89] and [TAY91]. Figure 2.2 represents those concepts using the graphic notation described in [MEY88]. In that notation, doughnut-shaped graphic elements represent the object data surrounded by its valid operations (access methods).

- **Object**

An **object** is a software "packet" containing a collection of data elements and a set of procedures that are the only valid operations on that data. Those operations are called *access methods*, *accessor methods,* or simply *methods.* Once defined, objects can be used as basic data types within a program.[1] An object has a *state,* presents an *interface,* and exhibits a *behavior.* The state is determined by the value of the object's internal data, which results from the operations performed on that data by changing its state. The variables representing the internal state of an object are called **instance variables.** The collection of methods determines the object's interface and behavior.

- **Class**

A **class** is a generalized description of the characteristics of similar objects. It is a template from which objects may be created by invoking certain methods associated with the class, usually called *create* or *new* methods.[2] As with objects, the operations of a class determine its behavior. Objects of the same class have common operations and therefore uniform behavior. Classes have one or more *interfaces* that specify the operations accessible to clients through that interface. A *class body* specifies code for implementing operations in the class interface.

- **Inheritance**

Inheritance is a code-sharing mechanism. It allows reuse of the behavior of a class in the definition of new classes. Subclasses of a class inherit the data structure and the operations of their parent class (also called a **superclass**) and may add new operations and new instance variables. Inheritance is often referred to as an "is-a" relationship: if the class A inherits from class B, then it is possible to say that A "is-a" B. Inheritance from a single superclass is called *single*

---

1. *A data structure with an associated set of operators, in which the implementation details are hidden, is called an* **abstract data type** *(ADT). ADTs allow the user to reference the abstract data objects with implementation-independent code.*

---

2. *An object is created from a class with precisely the same variables and operations as the class, but their interpretation is different: whereas the instance variables of an object represent actual variables, the class instance variables are potential, being instantiated only when an object is created.*

inheritance; inheritance from multiple superclasses is called *multiple inheritance*. Not all OOPLs support multiple inheritance.

The support for objects, classes, and inheritance is the distinguishing feature of an object-oriented system.

The terms *message, method, encapsulation*, and *polymorphism* are frequently used in the literature. Their meanings are as follows.

- **Message**

Messages are signals sent from one object to another that request the receiving object to carry out one of its methods. Messages are similar to function calls: they tell an object which service or state change it should perform.

- **Method**

Methods are procedures contained within an object that are executed in response to a message. Depending on the language, most or all of the communication between objects takes place by sending messages that invoke methods.

- **Encapsulation**

Encapsulation can be defined as a form of information hiding. It allows changes to be made to the implementation of a system with minimal effects on the end user. It is a technique by which data is packaged together with its corresponding procedures (methods). The state data in an object is said to be *encapsulated* from the outside world. This means that the internal data of an object can only be accessed through the message interface for that object. The way in which the internal data is accessed is hidden from the requester, because it is neither required nor convenient that the designer of the application should be aware of the internal implementation details of the method invoked by a message.

- **Polymorphism**

Polymorphism is a word of Greek origin that means *having multiple forms.* It refers to the ability to hide different implementations behind a common interface. With polymorphism, the same message can be interpreted differently by objects of different classes and therefore produce different but appropriate results. For example, the message *displayYourself* sent to a Circle object will result in a circle being drawn on the screen, whereas the same message sent to a Square or a Text should result in the square or the block of text appearing on the screen. Polymorphism allows methods to be written in a generic way and is therefore essential in facilitating reuse.

2.4 Benefits of Object Technology

Object technology provides the following benefits. Some are important to the end user, and others to the developer.

- Objects in the computer represent things in the real world and can therefore be designed to be manipulated in a way that is similar to the manipulation of real-world objects. Object-oriented techniques are thus particularly well suited to the development of today's complex user interfaces. Applications are becoming friendlier and easier to use. The same applies to the programming of objects: the technology allows users to communicate their requirements better and programmers to structure their programs in a more natural way.

- Object technology has the potential to reduce significantly the application maintenance load because of the inherent modularity and low coupling among object-oriented constructs provided by encapsulation. Each object presents to the world only its public interface; the inner works are hidden, and can be modified without rippling the effect of the modification to other modules. A key concept in object technology is that an application can be constructed from existing modules, also called *parts* or *components.* If those components are well tested, an application will be built with a large proportion of high-quality code to start with, and the maintenance load will be reduced. In addition, the identification of common parts among and within applications facilitates model and code reuse. Therefore, less coding is required, and so less coding errors are likely to be introduced: this reduces even further the maintenance requirements.

- The flexibility of object-oriented software allows for easy application prototyping, building, and changing in response to evolving requirements. The net result is that the application reflects a better understanding of the user requirements, and this leads to greater user satisfaction and productivity. In addition, fewer modifications are required after the application is released.

- Common functions in different applications can be provided by common, shared objects, leading to a more uniform and consistent user interface across the system as a whole. It is therefore possible that users may someday "start up applications as they start up their cars, with no more concern about the underlying structure of the objects they manipulate than the driver has about the molecular construction of gasoline" [OMG90].

- Conceptually, object orientation can offer uniformity throughout the whole application development life cycle. When using object technology, it is no longer necessary, for instance, to translate the data flow diagrams of the requirements phase to decision tables in the design phase, and then to PL/I code in the implementation phase.

2.5 Summary

- Object technology introduces the following key concepts: objects, classes, inheritance, encapsulation, and polymorphism.

- Object can be used to describe the user's real world. This facilitates the understanding of the user requirements.

- The key benefits of object technology are a better representation of the user's real world, reuse, uniformity, and increased productivity with enhancement of software quality. These benefits can contribute significantly to the successful exploitation of information technology within an enterprise.

3

Object-Oriented
Analysis and Design

The most recent advances in object technology have taken place in the areas of analysis and design. A number of authors who made their names in the development of structured methodologies are now involved in these areas of the new technology (for example, Paul Ward, Edward Yourdon, James Martin). In addition, the object-oriented literature has grown with the works of new authors, such as Sally Schlaer, Stephen Mellor, James Rumbaugh, Bertrand Meyer, Grady Booch, Ivar Jacobson, and Rebecca Wirfs-Brock, to name a few.

Practitioners of object technology generally agree that analysis and design are key activities that will ensure the success of medium- to large-sized application development projects. Nevertheless, experienced programmers who use an object-oriented programming language such as Smalltalk and work independently or in very small teams prefer to write code almost from the start of development, relying on thorough prototyping activity to capture the user's requirements.

This situation is not unique to object orientation. Usually, languages were developed before the theory of how to use them. First came unstructured programming, then structured programming, later structured design, and finally, structured analysis. A similar situation occurred with object orientation. The origin of the OOPLs is usually traced to the programming language Simula, developed in 1967 in Norway to handle simulations of complex real-world interactions. Simula 67 and LISP inspired the creation of several versions of the Smalltalk language, which were developed during the 1970s at Xerox's Palo Alto Research Center (PARC). Object-oriented design (OOD) methodologies emerged in the mid 1980s, and object-oriented analysis (OOA) began in the late 1980s. Therefore, in many organizations, such as corporations and universities, the approach to object technology started with using a language as a medium in which people could learn and explore the new paradigm.

In addition, the tools required to support the various methodologies are just starting to be available, and not all of them provide full function. The notation for modeling diagrams is usually rather complex, and without good tools redrawing on paper is time-consuming and cumbersome. Programmers hesitate to embrace a methodology with a complex notation on a project of any size without something easier to use and maintain than paper. (Regardless of whether CASE tools are properly exploited today, their ability to produce diagrams has come to be regarded as a prerequisite for using a methodology.)

3.1 Definitions

Broadly speaking, analysis is the process of describing the problem to be solved (the answer to the *what* question). From the same perspective, design is the process of describing the solution (the global answer to the *how* question), and programming is the process of implementing the solution (the detailed answer to the *how* question) [DUN92].

The characteristics of the analysis, design, and programming activities may vary with the application development life cycle approach. In the *conservative waterfall approach,* these activities take place in a strict sequence. In another approach, the programmer builds a prototype using objects that represent real-world "things," discusses the prototype with the user, and refines it until the user is satisfied. This process is called the *radical waterfall approach* [YOU92]: a waterfall life cycle in which the phases of analysis, design, coding, and testing are started approximately at the same time, and the user requirements are interpreted through the prototyping process. This approach is fine for very small or research-type projects, but for MIS team development of business applications, thinking ahead is essential.

The process of thinking ahead can be formalized by adopting a methodology[1] that guides the application development phases and the process of moving through the phases. Some of the leading books on the subject are [BOO92], [COA91a-b], [SHL88,91], [WIR90], and [RUM91].

Object-Oriented Modeling

In object technology, models of different levels of detail and depth are created in the analysis and design phases. Object-oriented analysis (OOA) is the analysis of a real-world system; the result is a model that comprises a number of objects. Each object in the model corresponds to an object in the real world; that is, there is a natural mapping from the problem domain to the model domain. Some of the objects of the model are obvious and easy to identify, but some are not. We call the objects identified in the domain analysis **semantic objects**, since these are the only meaningful ones from the domain point of view.

The analysis model is a concise, precise, abstraction of *what* the desired system must do, not *how* it should be done. The objects in the model should be application-domain concepts, and not programming concepts such as data structures. A good model can be understood and criticized by application experts who are not programmers [RUM91]. Since modeling is the main activity, OOA is often called *object-oriented modeling*.

Object-oriented design (OOD) is the design of a software system based on objects; it includes the translation into the software system of the overall software architecture and the data structures and algorithms of the main objects. It is natural for OOD to follow OOA, and severe problems can arise when doing an OOD without a previous OOA [LUK92]. During the design phase, new objects, not domain-derived but implementation-oriented, may be defined.

Figure 3.1 shows the relation between OOA and OOD. The semantic objects will be implemented as application objects. Additional objects such as interface and utility objects are required in this phase to complete a practical computer implementation.

Object-oriented programming achieves its maximum productivity when the coding phase is the implementation of an OOD in an object-

---

1. *In this publication the term* methodology *signifies a unified approach or set of steps applied to the process of analyzing problems and designing computer-based solutions. The term* method *is only used as an abbreviation of* object (class or instance) access method.

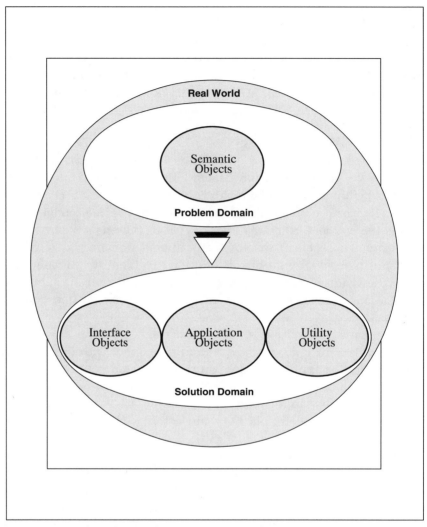

FIGURE 3.1 The relations between OOA and OOD

oriented programming language. It is important in the analysis and design phases not to be committed to a specific language, although this is more difficult in the latter phase. It may not always be feasible to use an object-oriented programming language, but there are still advantages to reap from the modularity inherent in a good OOA and OOD.

The object-oriented paradigm provides a seamless approach to application development. Because one set of concepts and notation can be used throughout the life cycle of the project, it becomes much easier to go from analysis to design and from design to implementation.

However, this makes it difficult sometimes to draw the line between the analysis and design phases. Depending on the purpose of the analysis work, whether it will be used in an integrated fashion with other analysis models, and whether it needs to be valid for a longer period of time, it may be desirable to keep a clear border between analysis and design, even somewhat artificially.

CRC Cards: A Technique for Class Design

A variety of design techniques for object-oriented applications have been developed. The use of CRC cards that we describe here was developed by Beck and Cunningham [BEC89]. It has been advocated both as an initial brainstorming aid and as a class design tool, which was the original intent of the authors. CRC stands for *class, responsibility, and collaborators,* and the CRC cards are index cards on which information about classes can be recorded (Figure 3.2).

Using one card per class, we register the names of the classes identified (e.g., Account), without making at this stage any particular distinctions between classes and objects. We also register the class responsibilities, that is, the problems to be solved by that class. This is best done in short, active verb phrases with only one verb per

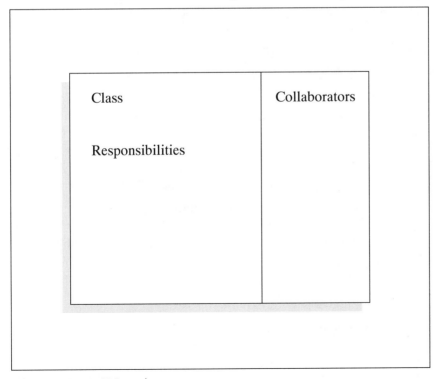

FIGURE 3.2   A CRC card

phrase (e.g., "Maintain the account balance"). The set of class responsibilities can be viewed as a contract to be fulfilled by the class.

The collaborators of a class are related classes that provide the services that allow the class to satisfy its contracted responsibilities. Defining for the class model the relationship of "who does what" is the first step in object-oriented design. CRC cards have been used extensively as a starting instrument for class modeling. In the experience of the authors of this book, they are also a very effective design tool when used after performing class modeling, which can be done in the way prescribed by any of the methodologies presented below.

Characteristics of Methodologies

An object-oriented analysis consists of a number of steps, as summarized below. The steps listed are synthesized from several authors, and thus any one of the texts referred to above may characterize and order them differently. The steps are intended to introduce the major tasks that will be encountered, whichever methodology is adopted.

1. Gather requirements.

2. Describe typical scenarios.

3. Identify candidate objects—what they are, what they are responsible for.

4. Establish relationships between objects and describe the required behavior.

5. Iterate.

The purpose of steps 1 through 5 is to establish a fairly complete description of the problem domain in terms of objects and the basic interactions among them. As is appropriate for analysis, the process makes no assumptions about the technology on which the system (or systems) will be implemented. The steps shade into those for design:

6. Refine the definition of the relationships to reflect object-oriented modeling concepts, such as aggregation (part-whole relationship), association (generic relationship), and inheritance.

7. Expand on internal details of objects, describing methods and variables.

8. Identify objects with existing classes.

9. Generalize the objects.

10. Iterate.

The purpose of steps 6 through 10 is to complete the definition of the objects in enough detail to avoid any ambiguity in their implementation. In this set of steps we are clearly adapting the output from the analysis to the requirements of the particular environment in which the system is to be implemented. We emphasize controlled iteration as a natural and effective ingredient of the application development life cycle that helps to achieve the required functionality and allows for a better interpretation and implementation of the user requirements. Note that although the steps appear sequentially, they could overlap in time, taking place concurrently.

3.2 The Need for Methodologies

For object technology to be productive in the development of complex or interactive systems, the use of a methodology is crucial for a number of reasons:

- Acceptance in the MIS environment. The application development methodologies that came into use over the past years have improved quality control by ensuring that the end product complies with the stated requirements. Increasing automation through the use of CASE tools does promise that the links from requirements definition through to system delivery will be made even stronger. Since the main reason to adopt object technology is productivity, it is easy to understand why formal OOA/OOD methodologies are required in the MIS environments.

- Large problem domains and large-scale designs. One of the purposes of any methodology is to ensure consistency and comprehensiveness in the analysis and design phase. Thus, a methodology can be considered as a management tool. Object orientation focuses on more things than structured analysis does, because it is concerned with more than just the immediate problem. One of the main reasons for the productivity gains provided by object-oriented systems is the exploitation of existing designs and code through reuse. That additional complexity requires additional control.

- Documentation requirements. It is difficult to understand an object-oriented system by looking only at the code of the classes that it comprises. This applies to both the purpose of the application and the way it functions. The models that result from a good methodology are essential to the documentation of the project. For example, an object model defines the classes, and a message flow diagram shows how classes collaborate to achieve particular application requirements.

3.3 Structured Analysis Methodologies

Object technologies entail a paradigm shift, and thus there are many requirements, based on investment and human factors, for a smooth transition during the shift process. So, to the question "Can existing structured analysis methodologies still be used?" the answer is "Yes and no." Investment that has been made in building models, learning techniques for analysis, and becoming acquainted with CASE tools will not be wasted, but structured methodologies alone do not cover sufficient ground for the requirements of object-oriented application development.

At present, structured methodologies use a number of the following techniques:

- Functional (or process) decomposition
- Entity-relationship (E-R) modeling
- Data flow diagramming
- Event (or control) flow diagramming
- State-transition analysis
- Prototyping screens

Some of these techniques are still useful for object-oriented application development, but others are not. The structured techniques are described below and positioned relative to object technology.

Functional Decomposition

The familiar top-down approach is implemented in analysis and design most commonly as a form of functional decomposition. The problem here is that this approach starts from the concept that the system under analysis represents a single function, which can be broken down into successive levels of detail as one moves through the analysis process. The functions are identified as components of a process that combine to address the particular problem at hand. Data is described, using data flow diagrams, in terms of its movement among these functions. Figure 3.3 shows an example of a functional decomposition diagram.

As already discussed, object orientation emphasizes an evolutionary approach to all phases of the development process. Assuming

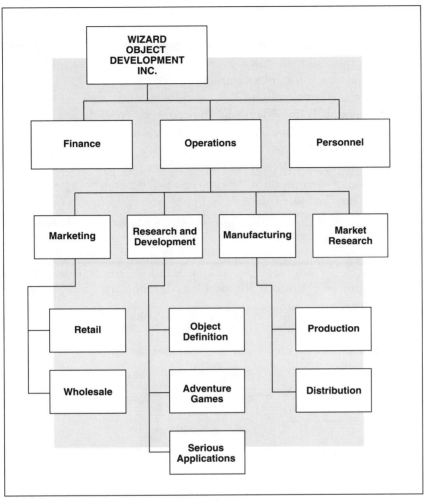

FIGURE 3.3   Functional decomposition diagram

that requirements will not change (and that therefore the system can be frozen as a single, all-encompassing functional description at the top level) is not realistic. Thinking of the components of an application only in relation to the other components in a particular context is not sufficient. It does not help us to understand what the components *are* (as opposed to understanding what they *do*), which is essential to identifying objects. If there is no requirement to think of what an object *is,* there is even less of a requirement to think of what it *is like*, and therefore possibilities for reuse are likely to be missed. Functional decomposition practiced on a large scale should therefore be avoided as part of an object-oriented methodology.

Entity-Relationship Modeling

Another important aspect of analysis that is often associated with structured analysis methodologies is derived from the information engineering technique—the E-R model. This model can make a significant contribution to object-oriented analysis.

Most of the entities in an E-R model are candidates for classes in an object model. If the E-R design has gone so far as to define attributes (often the step before producing a normalized relational database design), those attributes may prove to be a reasonable match for instance data. Figure 3.4 shows an example of an E-R diagram.

The degree of compatibility between E-R diagramming and object modeling can be seen in Rumbaugh's object-modeling technique (OMT) methodology. In [RUM91], the author states that "OMT object modeling is . . . an enhanced form of E-R." Indeed an entity model can be transformed into an (incomplete) object model with relative ease.

Although E-R techniques can be used in the analysis of the business area and even the specific problem domain, they have a number of drawbacks:

- By themselves, they only show a static view of the system.

- They do not describe abstractions and inheritance.

- They do not indicate the relation between the access methods

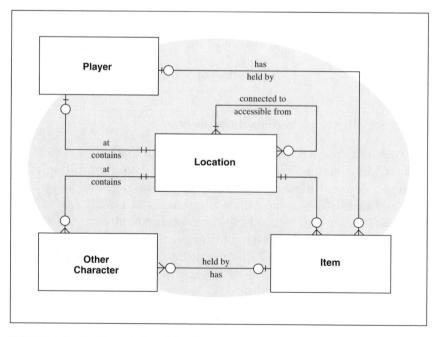

FIGURE 3.4   Entity-relationship diagram

and the data structures (that is, they do not describe encapsulation).

- They do not describe event-related information.
- They do not provide information about the user interface.

Other models or techniques are required to show objects "in the round."

Data Flow Diagramming

A data flow diagram (DFD) describes the flow of data in a system, where the data is stored, and how it is communicated to and from the outside world. In particular, DFDs can be used to find stores of data in the problem domain. Figure 3.5 shows an example of a data flow diagram, drawn using the notation similar to the one defined by Gane and Sarson [GAS89].

Although frequently used in functional analysis, DFDs are not useful in OOA. It is important to establish message flows between

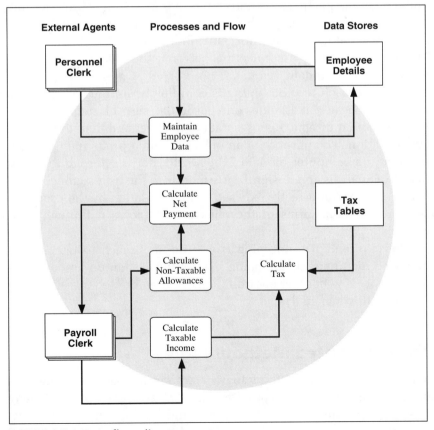

FIGURE 3.5   Data flow diagram

objects, and these may bear a superficial resemblance to DFDs. However, it should be clear by now that the idea of data *flowing* between objects does not fit well with object-oriented concepts. Objects encapsulate data, and only messages flow between objects.

It is possible to think of building DFDs and then transforming them into an object model. However, most authors seem to agree that this is difficult. Certainly there is no easy mapping between nodes in a DFD and objects. Some authors have, however, shown how pieces of an object (that is, data and the functions associated with that data) might be distributed widely throughout a design that has been constructed using DFDs.

Prototyping

Prototyping that is based on structured analysis does not have the same meaning as prototyping from an object-oriented modeling. The former consists largely of validating the design of the data. For example, a number of screens might be designed to be accessed through hierarchical menus (perhaps derived from the decomposition of functions in the system), on which fields appear that link directly to relational tables defined via an entity-attribute-relationship (EAR) model. The screen is simply a connection between the data and the user's desire to read or update that data.

This approach to prototyping is completely antithetical to object orientation because it assumes one particular view of underlying textual data, and it directly exposes data to the user and therefore breaks encapsulation. The purpose of an object-oriented prototype is to confirm that the computer model of the world, derived through various phases of analysis and design, corresponds to the user's model of the world. Data is not directly exposed to manipulation by the user; it is only presented in terms of the objects and accessed through their methods.

Object-oriented prototyping is a strong approach to testing that the user's requirements are being met by the system under construction. Prototyping in other environments is often limited merely to validation of the data analysis.

3.4 Object-Oriented Methodologies

Is it important for the methodology to support message flow diagramming or partitioned subtypes (to take just two examples of many possible techniques), or is the extent and comprehensibility of its documentation more significant? Experience with CASE tools and associated modeling methodologies tends to point toward the latter. The environment within which the methodology exists—its number of users, tool support, ease of acquisition—certainly influences buying decisions more than some of the more abstract advantages of the rigor of the methodology and the comprehensiveness of its notation.

It is useful to inject a note of caution into this pragmatic approach, however. Object orientation provides a cleaner interface between the design and implementation phases of a system. Certainly the code that is produced bears more resemblance to its associated E-R diagram than does any functional code. As the industry moves further toward code generation as the direct output of the process of designing and refining business models, it becomes important for the model to capture more and more detail of the world it describes in order to ensure that the code produced fully reflects that world. Thus, the subtle gradations of completeness between one modeling methodology and another may come to have more than academic interest.

A number of papers (e.g., [FOW91], [CHA92]) have attempted to compare current methodologies, but as long as there is little feedback from using the methodologies in development projects of any significant size, such comparisons are likely to focus only on academic strengths and weaknesses. What is put forward below is an assertion of the function that any methodology must have in order to be useful, and suggestions for the criteria that could be used to select a methodology.

The following steps were identified earlier in this chapter as common to object-oriented analysis and design:

1. Gather requirements.

2. Describe typical scenarios.

3. Identify candidate objects—what they are, what they know.

4. Establish relationships between objects and describe the desired behavior.

5. Iterate.

6. Refine the definition of the relationships to reflect the object-oriented concepts of aggregation, collaboration, and inheritance.

7. Expand on internal details of objects, describing methods and variables.

8. Identify objects with existing classes.

9. Generalize the objects.

10. Iterate.

To support this process, a methodology must be capable of expressing in some way all the basic object-oriented concepts and portraying both the dynamic and static aspects of any set of objects (see following). Methodologies may differ in their approach: for instance, the order of steps 3 and 4 will vary depending on whether a behavior-driven or data-driven methodology is adopted (see following).

The static aspects are best described in an object model, which shows the objects in the system and how they relate to other objects. The object model differs from an E-R model in its level of abstraction (it should provide ways of representing abstract superclasses) and its specification of the inheritance relation. The object model should also be able to represent the encapsulating structure of an object, that is, what its methods and variables are.

Dynamic aspects are best expressed by an analysis of the behavior of objects. The most important point is to know which objects have to collaborate in order to achieve a goal. Use cases (see the discussion of OOSE, p.41), or scenarios, provide the input to both the class and the dynamic model, and specific instances of user or system interactions can be usefully illustrated by message flow diagrams. Such diagrams also provide sample test cases for the system.

Static and Dynamic Modeling

Any analysis and design methodology usually consists of one or more modeling techniques [FOW91]. Each methodology focuses on certain aspects of the system and therefore emphasizes one technique over the others. For example, one methodology may have a main technique for modeling and use the other techniques as refining procedures. The emphasis can also be placed by enforcing one technique as a starting point for defining objects, in which case the results of modeling with one or another methodology may be quite different. The main currents of OOA and OOD can be characterized as the *data-driven* or *static* methodologies, and the *behavior-driven* or *dynamic* methodologies, also called by some authors *responsibility-driven* methodologies [WIR89].

In a static methodology, objects are defined by focusing on the data structure the object represents and on the operations that can be performed on that object. An object is therefore defined in a static methodology because it represents an interesting or important data structure.

In a dynamic methodology, an object is defined because it represents an entity that exhibits an interesting behavior. This behavior can be referred to the object itself; it is then characterized by the changes of states of its internal variables when the object is affected by certain events. The behavior can also be referred to the object's relation with other objects in the model. The objects are perceived as cooperating and collaborating agents that have responsibilities following closely the client/server model. Another view adds the notion of behavioral scripts [GIB90], derived from techniques used in artificial intelligence for natural-language processing.

Another important aspect is the design of the algorithms underlying the operations of the objects; some methodologies include this aspect as part of their techniques. In addition, the overall architectural view is sometimes defined as a design template [SHL91]. In other cases techniques such as data flow diagrams are used to determine the functional decomposition of the system, although the object-oriented approach suggests that decomposing by aggregation rather than by function may be more appropriate. Five object-oriented modeling methodologies and the deliverables they define for the analysis process are described below.

Object-Oriented Design (Grady Booch)

Grady Booch's object-oriented design (OOD) methodology [BOO92] is based on a structuring principle that favors object-oriented decomposition over functional decomposition. OOD focuses more on design issues than on the analysis process. It emphasizes the need for the design process to produce multiple views (different models) in order to capture all of the design decisions that must be made. However, the deliverables of OOD include the static and dynamic models we have considered.

The methodology prescribes the creation of a logical view of the object model that depicts the class and object structure and relationships, without any implementation constraints. Creation of the logical view occurs during the analysis phase. In the design phase, the model is refined to take into account implementation considerations. The resulting physical view of the model captures the design decisions for later implementation. The OOD methodology assumes that during the application development life cycle, the analysis and design phases are traversed iteratively and incrementally, augmenting formal diagrams with informal documentation techniques.

OOD delineates four major steps during the modeling process; there is no prescription to follow these steps in a fixed order.

- Identify classes and objects at a given level of abstraction. A domain analysis is performed to find the key abstractions (classes). As part of the domain analysis, class templates are filled out, documenting the classes found.

- Identify the semantics of classes and objects. The responsibilities of the classes are determined in an iterative way. A script is written for each object in the application, describing its life cycle from creation to destruction, including its characteristic behaviors. The deliverables from this step are refined templates drafted in the first step.

- Identify the relationships among classes and objects. This step is required to establish the interactions among classes and to identify inheritance relationships. Two related activities help to refine the design arrived at during the second step: the discovery of patterns and the determination of visibility decisions. OOD identifies two types of patterns: patterns among classes, which help us to recognize and simplify the model's class structure, and patterns among cooperative collections of objects, which lead to a generalization of the mechanisms already embodied in the design. Visibility decisions determine how classes (and objects) should see one another, which affects the design of the architecture of the target system. Booch suggests using the technique of class-responsibility-collaboration (CRC) cards in this step.

- Implement classes and objects. Design decisions are made during this step, including allocation of modules and processors.

Diagrams

Booch describes a variety of representations, notations, and techniques to assist in object-oriented design, including the use of formal and informal diagrams and templates.

Some of those diagrams are described below.

- Class diagram. Shows classes and their relationships, such as inheritance, instantiation, utilization, and metaclass.

- Object diagram. Used to model the dynamics of objects. Shows individual objects and their message connections. Figure 3.6 provides an example.

- State-transition diagram. Depicts the state of a class, the events that cause transition from one state to another, and the actions that result from a state change.

- Timing diagram. Shows flow of control and ordering of events among a group of collaborating objects.

- Module diagram. Documents the physical packaging of classes into modules.

- Process diagram. Shows the allocation of processes to processors.

Object-Oriented Software Engineering (Ivar Jacobson)

The object-oriented software engineering (OOSE) methodology [JAC92] introduces the notion of *use cases*. A use case comprises a course of events begun by an actor, and it specifies the interaction between the actor and the rest of the system. All use cases specify existing ways to use the whole system.

- Objects correspond to the nouns of the problem domain. The main difficulty is to be sure that a noun is relevant to the domain and not to the design, or even to another domain. Jacobson recommends grouping nouns according to such characteristics as active/passive, private/public, and temporary/permanent.

- The classification of objects is required to obtain the class hierarchy. Finding similarities in objects is the first step in the inheritance classification.

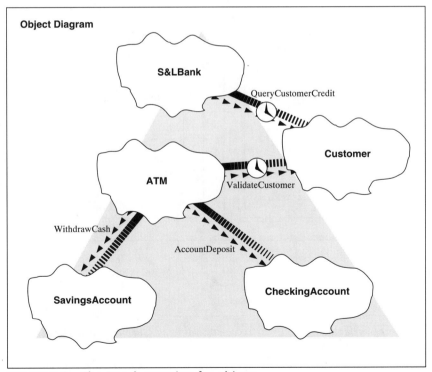

FIGURE 3.6   The Booch notation for objects

- Use cases define how objects interact and communicate. They represent scenarios that describe what each object can expect from other objects; this defines the object's interface. Structural relationships among objects, such as which objects are part of other objects, can also be determined.

- Operations on objects are defined by the objects' interfaces. They can be simple (e.g., add, delete) or more complex, in which case new objects can be found.

- Finally, the structure of an object is defined by the information that it must contain.

As a result of applying the OOSE methodology, we get the six models shown in Figure 3.7. These models describe the use cases, the application domain, and the analysis, design, implementation, and testing of the application.

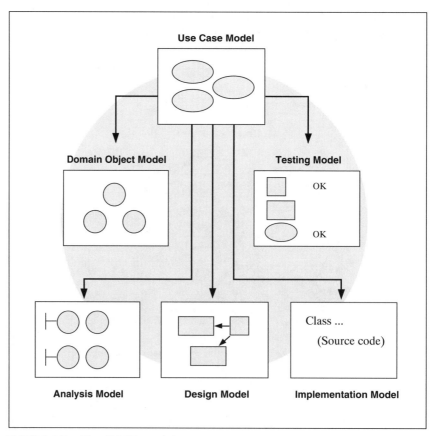

FIGURE 3.7   The OOSE models

The Object-Modeling Technique (OMT)
(James Rumbaugh et al.)

The object-modeling technique (OMT) is a comprehensive methodology that consists of several phases [RUM91]. We will describe briefly the outstanding features of OMT, which reside mainly in its approach to analysis and design.

- *Analysis*

The analysis phase is concerned with understanding and modeling the application and the domain within which it operates. The initial input to the analysis phase is a problem statement that describes the problem to be solved and provides a conceptual overview of the proposed system. Subsequent dialog with the customer and real-world background knowledge provide additional inputs to analysis.

The output from analysis is a formal model (see Figure 3.8) that captures what this methodology considers the three essential aspects of the system: (1) the objects and their relationships, (2) the dynamic flow of control, and (3) the functional transformation of data subject to constraints. In addition, a data dictionary is built: this document describes each object class with its scope, assumptions and restrictions. The data dictionary also describes associations, attributes, and operations.

- *Design*

There are two phases of design: *system design* and *object design*. The goal of the system design phase is to determine the overall architecture. This is done by organizing the system into subsystems, using the object model as a guide. In the object design phase, the emphasis shifts from application concepts to computer concepts. The designer chooses the basic algorithms to implement each major function of the system, optimizes the structure of the object model, and determines the implementation of the relationships among objects (called *associations)* and of the objects' attributes.

OMT promotes a shifting of the development effort to the analysis phase of the life cycle. It can be considered a static methodology because data structure is emphasized more than function. The authors consider that this emphasis on data structure gives the development process a more stable base, because the data structures of an application and the relationships among them are much less vulnerable to changing requirements than are the operations performed on the data.

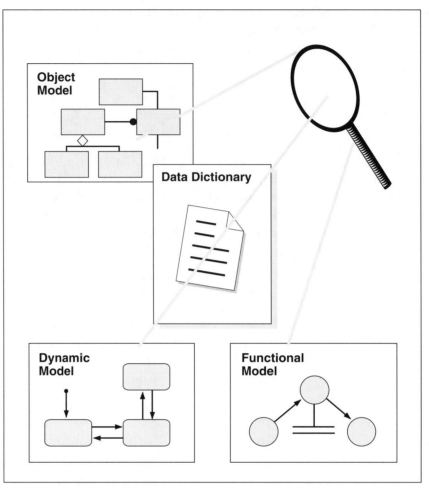

FIGURE 3.8   The OMT models

Responsibility-Driven Design (Rebecca Wirfs-Brock)

Dynamic, or behavioral, approaches stem from the basic notion that an object encapsulates behavior. According to some authors [WAS92], the behavioral approach seems to provide better support for data abstraction, modularity, and information hiding than does the data-modeling approach.

The responsibility-driven design approach, developed by Rebecca Wirfs-Brock et al., is a dynamic methodology that emphasizes the encapsulation of both the structure and behavior of objects [WIR 89, WIR90]. It does so by viewing a program in terms of the client/server model, which describes the interaction between two entities: the client and the server. A client requests the server to perform services.

A server provides a set of services upon request. The ways in which the client can interact with the server are described by a *contract.* Both must fulfill the contract: the client by making only those requests it specifies, and the server by responding to those requests.

In object-oriented programming, both client and server are classes or instances of classes. Client and server are roles played by the objects: any object can be either a client or a server at any given time.

In the responsibility-driven design approach, the analysis phase is called the *initial exploratory phase* [WIR90]. This phase involves identifying the objects based on their behavior; determining their *responsibilities,* that is, what each individual object will do to help the system attain its goal; and establishing *collaborations* among objects, that is, determining the other objects that each object cooperates with in order to accomplish its responsibilities (Figure 3.9). Responsibilities and collaborations also define the knowledge that an object must have in order to accomplish each of its goals, including the definition of other objects in the system that either hold the knowledge the object needs or know how to perform some operation it requires.

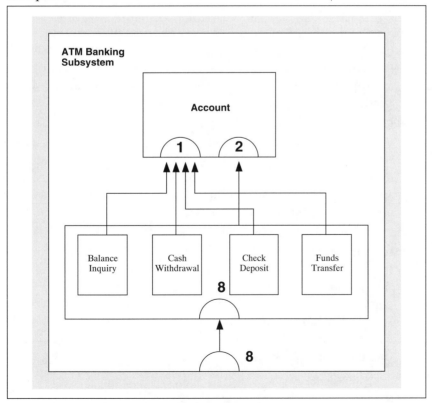

FIGURE 3.9   A Wirfs-Brock collaborations graph

At the end of the design process, objects become clients and servers within a system, responsibilities become contracts between them, and collaborations determine which clients and which servers are bound by contracts. The contracts are defined by the set of requests a client can make of a server. For each such request, a set of signatures serves as the formal specification of the contract. (A *signature* is a specification of the input to and the output from a method). A client/server contract promotes the reusability of server code, because a new user object (client) knows by the provider's (server's) contract specifications the responsibilities it has to fulfill [HEL90].

Responsibility-driven design is a dynamic methodology because it specifies object behavior before object structure and other considerations are determined. The authors of this methodology believe that it minimizes the rework required by major design changes [WIR89].

Object-Behavior Analysis (OBA) (ParcPlace Systems)

Object-behavior analysis (OBA) is a dynamic methodology based on the use of scripts, object-modeling cards, and glossaries. It includes the following steps.

- Set the context. Setting the context consists of identifying goals (the reasons for building a system) and objectives (measurable descriptions of every key aspect of the project, such as quality), appropriate resources for analysis, core activity areas, and a preliminary analysis plan.

- Determine the system objectives. The second step determines what the system is supposed to do, and for whom and with whom it is supposed to do it. *Use scenarios* are created to describe all pathways through the system functions. These are similar to the use cases defined by Jacobson in OOSE. Scripts are used to describe actions between an agent and a recipient, a sender object and a receiver, and the results of the actions.

- Identify analysis objects. Analysis objects are identified by using scripts. Object-modeling are created to capture information related to one object. These are similar to CRC cards. They contain the name of the object, the names of the objects from which attributes and behaviors are inherited, attributes and behaviors added by the object, and services provided and contracted by the object.

- Classify objects. The object modeling cards provide the basis for a classification of the objects. The goal is to find similar behaviors among several objects, to find services or logical properties of objects that can be described as refinements of the services and properties of another object, and to find objects whose multiple responsibilities can be split by creating new objects for each area of responsibility. These techniques are known as *abstraction, generalization*, and *aggregation.*

- Provide a dynamic view of the system. This step is concerned with all aspects of the system that change over time. The OBA methodology uses state glossaries to describe the life cycle of objects, that is, how objects move from state to state in response to events.

Multiple Methodologies and Notations

Although the order of steps may not the be the same, following one or another methodology produces similar deliverables in different notations: a class model, describing the object classes (with their names, attributes, methods, and relations), and a behavior model, describing the behavior of the model objects in prototypical scenarios. Different modeling approaches, however, produce models with different characteristics, even though the models are of the same type. For instance, two different methodologies may produce class diagrams populated with classes of different names, or with the same names but different attributes and operations. Rebecca Wirfs-Brock [WIR92] illustrates this point with the following example.

Assume that the problem is to model a horse. Different modeling approaches might describe the horse in different ways.

- A *data-driven* approach would describe a horse in terms of its *parts:*

      head, tail, body, and legs(4)

- A *procedure-driven* approach would describe a horse in terms of the *operations* it can perform:

      walk, run, trot, eat, bite

- An *event-driven* approach would describe a horse in terms of the external *events* it processes:

      rider mount, rider dismount, pulling the
      reins, leg cues

- A *responsibility-driven* approach would describe a horse in terms of its *responsibilities:*

```
carry a rider to a destination, run a race
```

To extend this example, we may compare the data-driven modeling approach with the responsibility-driven approach when modeling a horse-and-carriage transport. A data-driven approach would most probably identify two classes, Horse and Carriage, linked by an association, such as *Draws* or *Drawn_by*. A responsibility-driven methodology may suggest the advantage of modeling a Horse-and-Carriage class, because for this application, neither the horse nor the carriage alone can fulfill its responsibilities.

Ideally, an organization would standardize on a given methodology and its corresponding notation. Reality shows [GOL92], however, that many organizations develop their own in-house methodology (sometimes derived from a published discipline) and choose a certain notation, whose semantics may or may not coincide with its author's original intent. In addition, given the current trends in downsizing, different departments of large organizations often embrace different methodologies. This does not mean that cross-enterprise reuse is impossible under such circumstances, but it does place an additional burden on the enterprise's reuse organization.

3.5 Additional Requirements for an Object-Oriented Methodology

From an integrated application development point of view, a number of issues are not fully addressed in the better-known object-oriented methodologies as they are currently defined. One problem is the need for a more detailed and comprehensive approach to the analysis and design of the user interface components of an application. The published methodologies do not address thoroughly the need to design views and perhaps even additional classes for the interface in addition to the other objects in the system. In terms of the model-view-controller paradigm, object-oriented analysis and design appear to be concentrating mainly on the model part. As is discussed further in Chapter 6, "Team and Project Implementation Issues," this may happen because most developers who produce the model objects usually work with different tools and techniques than those used by the developers who deal with the view and controller.

The proportion of the whole development effort that is involved in designing and building the user interface is often greater than would be expected. The most useful general approach to interface building is found in methodologies that use event-driven design frameworks and state diagrams, such as OMT [RUM91]. Of course, this problem is not specific to object technology. Building a complex user interface is a problem in any application development technology. The reason for the need to address this problem in a more systematic way is rooted in the attractiveness of object technology for end users: the object-action paradigm. (Chapter 5, "The User Interface and Visual Programming," assesses the issues involved in designing and building object-oriented user interfaces.)

The result is that it is possible to invest in a methodology, use it to analyze, design, and implement a powerful set of model objects, and still find that a significant amount of work must be done before finishing the applications according to user expectations. This is not an argument, however, for ignoring the advantages of building the model: a good user interface must be built on a sound foundation of model objects. The visual programming tools now appearing on the market, such as IBM's VisualAge,™ combined with a prototyping approach to requirements gathering, can provide a practical solution for building rapidly a satisfactory interface and coupling it to the model.

A different problem is integrating the object-oriented models with the enterprise model and relating them to the business processes. Most methodologies do not use an enterprise or business-area model as a starting point for the object model. They approach the development process from a perspective that is neither top-down nor bottom-up but middle-out, that is, at the real-world level of the application. The models used in most of the object-oriented methodologies do not consider integration aspects explicitly, except for reusability issues. But enterprise modeling uses other models, which reflect different levels of abstraction, for different purposes within the business.

Existing models, especially at an abstract level, can provide useful initial input for the process of object analysis and modeling, because work that has been done at the business-area level remains valid. Thus, existing entity-relationship or entity-attribute-relationship diagrams in the problem domain can provide a base for creating the object models.

Another issue that has not yet been addressed is the need for CASE tools to support iteration. This means that there must be a complete closed loop of information from the upper-CASE level to the lower-CASE level, and from there to the execution environment and back. Before existing designs and code can be reused iteratively, higher-level tools must be able to understand them.

3.6 Summary

The foregoing discussion leads to the following conclusions with regard to object-oriented analysis and design.

- Modeling is important. It can become the primary source of documentation for the system and its objects.

- Analysis at a high level, for the enterprise and business area, can still be done with traditional E-R tools, although this offers a static view of the enterprise and its processes. Object-oriented technology could be used in this activity by performing a generalization process starting from the real-world models and going to application frameworks and from there to business-area and enterprise modeling. Simulation techniques for enterprise modeling could also be applied.

- If structural models exist, either at an enterprise or application level, then it is beneficial to use them, but the transformation is not direct.

- Which object-oriented modeling methodology is chosen is probably not significant, as long as it can express the basic object-oriented concepts. It should be able to model objects that encapsulate data and function, inheritance between classes, and messages as the interface between objects. It should be able to specify the relationships of inheritance, association, and aggregation between objects. It should consider the dynamic as well as the static elements of an object-oriented system.

- Modeling is part of the spiral development process. The models are refined as the development progresses. It is not necessary to have a fully specified model before beginning to prototype.

- Existing structured analysis CASE tools should not be used without caution on objects. It is important to keep in mind that entities and objects, however similar in appearance, are different in nature.

4

Application Implementation in Object Technology

In this chapter we look at the application implementation process in an object-oriented environment as a stage of a process that starts with modeling, continues with design and then implementation, and under an iterative or spiral approach, goes back to the beginning stage. We consider the role of prototypes and interaction with users. Then we examine two object-oriented programming languages, Smalltalk and C++, comparing their characteristics and use. We also consider the role of CASE tools and their relation to object technology.

The importance of the modeling process in object-oriented application development underscores the need for adequate object oriented CASE tools. In the last part of this chapter we discuss the requirements for these tools and describe the features in the products currently available .

4.1 The Road to Implementation

The object-oriented modeling process extracts the appropriate abstractions from the problem domain, organizing them into classes. Not all of the classes are tangible entities; many represent useful concepts, such as an account or a transaction. Some of the classes encapsulate essential features about the problem domain and can therefore be reused in future applications.

Object-oriented design transforms the domain abstractions into implementable classes, although not all classes come from the domain, and not all the domain abstractions appear in the design directly as classes. A good naming scheme allows for continuity from the model to the design.

Object-oriented programming (OOP) converts the design classes into programs. These are organized as collaborating collections of classes, many of which can be members of a hierachy of classes related by inheritance.

Any application development activity may benefit from the use of a repository that stores the results of one development phase for use by the next one. CASE tools are then used in the development process both for modeling and for accessing the repository.

Figure 4.1 shows the role of the different components in the road from modeling to implementation. The input comes from the real-world characteristics and from user requirements. The output is the completed application. The repository of reusable components plays a key role in the productivity of the process.

Prototyping

The spiral and iterative approaches allow for application prototyping, the goal of which is to ensure that the developed application meets the real needs of the user, which are not always truly captured by a specification document. During prototyping, the developer should interact with users and domain experts as much as possible. The prototypes help to show proof of concept and stimulate feedback about real requirements.

There are two types of prototypes:

- *Analysis prototype*. The analysis prototype is an aid for exploring the problem domain. It is meant to inform the user and show proof of concept, not to be used as a basis for development. It should be discarded when it has served its purpose, and the final product should use the concepts exposed by the prototype, not its code.[1]

---

1. *The prototype code can obviously be used for other prototypes, if appropriate.*

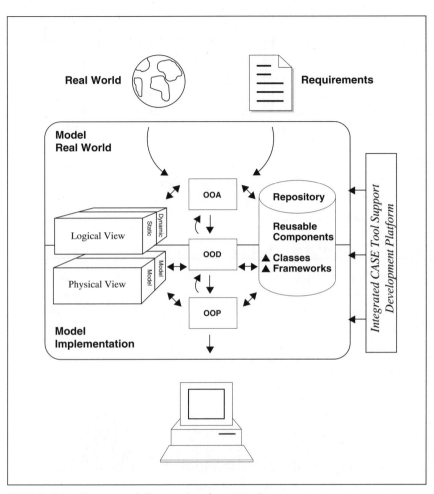

FIGURE 4.1   From modeling to implementation

- ***Domain prototype***. The domain prototype is an aid for the incremental implementation of the solution. It can be used as a tool for staged delivery of subsystems to users and other teams. It shows the feasibility of the implementation, and will eventually evolve into a deliverable product after testing, documentation, code cleanup, and review.

A major advantage of prototyping is that it promotes interaction among different groups such as users, domain experts, developers, planners, and managers. It helps everyone to understand the requirements and fosters team spirit. What is more important, it shows that concrete progress has been achieved.

The disadvantages of prototyping may derive from scaling problems. This occurs when a prototype behaves well in a limited domain, but the final product does not perform well under real-world conditions or under stress. Another problem is that developers may spend too much time iterating uncontrollably, trying all possible permutations in what Peter Dimitrios has called "a waltz through the solution space." In addition, the pressure both by management and by the user to ship a working prototype before it is sufficiently robust can be irresistible.

If the investment in object technology is to be worthwhile, it is essential to have an adequate development environment with the proper languages and tools. The next sections deal with these issues.

4.2   Object-Oriented Programming Languages

Object technology had its start in the field of programming, with the creation of the *Simula* simulation programming language in the late 1960s. There are now many object-oriented programming languages (OOPLs) in the marketplace, including Eiffel, Smalltalk-80, Smalltalk/V, C++, Actor, Objective-C, and CLOS. In addition, extensions to traditional languages, such as an object-oriented COBOL, are expected to be available soon.

Currently, the most popular languages for object-oriented programming are Smalltalk and C++. They come in many versions. The C++ versions are closer to each other, since there is an ANSI standard for C++. There is no standard for Smalltalk, although some efforts in that direction are under way. The following sections provide a general description of Smalltalk and C++.

Smalltalk

Smalltalk is an object-oriented development system that is available on most computing platforms. For instance, Smalltalk/V by Digitalk is available in versions that run under the OS/2 Presentation Manager, Microsoft Windows,™ and DOS. With minor modifications, Smalltalk/V source code is portable across platforms, and Smalltalk/V provides both a development environment and an execution service for each of the platforms.

The first version of Smalltalk was created by a research team at Xerox Corporation in the early 1970s. The Smalltalk language has currently a number of dialects that share the same concepts, although there are some differences both in the notation and the class hierarchy. Current dialects include IBM Smalltalk, Smalltalk-80, Enfintalk,

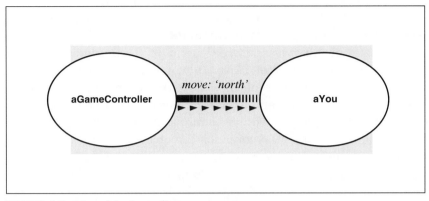

FIGURE 4.2   An object sending a message

and Smalltalk/V. In this book all the examples are written in the Smalltalk/V PM version for OS/2 Presentation Manager by Digitalk.

Smalltalk appears to differ little in its details from any other programming language. Thus, the syntax includes assignments, arithmetical expressions, conditional loop statements, and most of the constructs available in a modern computer language. Smalltalk differs from other programming languages in the way it builds up these small units of function into discrete objects. In Smalltalk everything is an object, and all work is carried out through messages. There are no built-in operators with fixed definitions.

The language implements the object-oriented paradigm directly; that is, the programming task follows the process of thinking conceptually about objects that are created from classes. Their behavior is manifested by the execution of the associated methods. These methods are triggered by *events,* which are the messages sent from one object to another.

The Game example presented in this book includes a class called GameController, which controls the movement of the characters that participate in the game. One of these characters is created from the class You and represents the player. Figure 4.2 shows an object created from the GameController class sending a message to an object, an instance of the You class, telling it to move in a specified direction.

In Smalltalk code, this can be expressed as

```
player:= You new.
player move: 'north'.
```

which can be interpreted as "create a new instance of the class You and store it in the variable called *player.*"[2] (In Smalltalk/V the

2. *In Smalltalk, the data is not actually stored in the variable. The variable contains a pointer to the data, not the data itself*

convention is that instance and temporary variable names start with lowercase letters and class names with uppercase letters.) Send the message *move* with argument *'north'* to that instance.

The result of this message will depend on the implementation of the *move:* method in the You class,[3] to which a YOU object stored in player responds. Smalltalk objects can only communicate via messages that invoke valid methods of each object, so in order to understand that message, You must have a *move:* method. This method can be implemented in the class to which the object corresponds, or in a superclass of the hierarchy to which it belongs. In the example, You is a subclass of a class called GameCharacter, and the *move:* method is implemented in the latter. Because You is a subclass, it inherits the methods of its superclass, so the message *move:* sent to an instance of You will be understood by that instance.

There is a justification for choosing to implement a method at the superclass level. In this program, which corresponds to the Game example, many intervening characters are represented by figures. The You class is used to generate an object, aYou, that represents the character identified with the player. Additional characters may be included in the script of the game, some controlled by the game itself, some by external events, and some even by other players (if the game can handle many players).

The Game example includes two subclasses of GameCharacter—You and OtherCharacter. The class of GameCharacter is called an *abstract class;* no instances of it exist, only instances of its subclasses. GameCharacter represents a generalization modeling option used to implement common behavior that is a characteristic of all its subclasses. Movement is one example of such common behavior.

Smalltalk/V is more than just a language. It is a complete environment, supported by a class library, a debugger, variable inspector, and most important, a browser. In Smalltalk/V the bulk of the application development takes place within the Class Hierarchy Browser window. This multipaned window, illustrated in Figure 4.3, shows the interrelationship of classes and subclasses and allows the editing of their associated variables and methods. As each method is saved, an incremental compilation of the code takes place, and any errors are immediately highlighted. This compilation process produces a compiled method, which is a sequence of *byte codes*. Byte codes are not machine instructions; a byte code interpreter executes the code at run time.

---

3. *The colon in* move: *indicates that this is a method that takes an argument.*

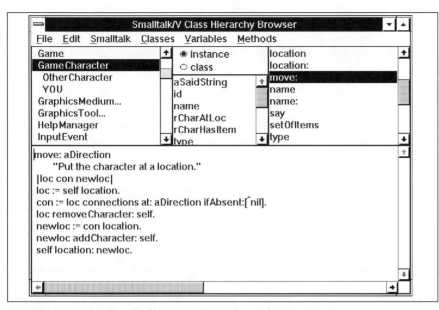

FIGURE 4.3   The Smalltalk/V PM Class Hierarchy Browser

The Smalltalk developer saves the application, together with the development environment, in an image. The Smalltalk image (that is, a module into which all code is compiled) is thus always legal code. This does not mean, however, that any application will always run successfully. The code is dynamically bound at run time, which means that type violations or other errors may only be discovered at that time. Smalltalk is a weakly typed language: the variables are not defined as having a specific type, such as integer or float, to be bound statically at compile time. Variables in Smalltalk do not usually contain data, but pointers to other objects, which are identified at run time. Therefore, the binding of a variable to a data type is determined at run time. This mechanism is called *late* or *dynamic* binding.

The left-hand pane of the Class Hierarchy Browser window in Figure 4.3 shows the Class Hierarchy. The indentation indicates that You is a subclass of GameCharacter. The variables for instances of this class are displayed in the middle pane, for instance, *id* and *name.* The right-hand pane shows the complete list of GameCharacter's methods. The highlighted *move:* method has its text displayed in the bottom pane. The code shows that GameCharacter is changing the state of the instance variables to reflect the new position of a character, having first checked whether or not the move is allowed.

Another element of Smalltalk/V that contributes to programming productivity is a class library, which is a standard part of the product. It is a comprehensive set that covers most of the basic classes, such as

Collection, Integer, and Window classes, that are needed to start building applications.

C++

C++ is an example of the evolution of a standard language to which object-oriented constructs have been added. The underlying language in this case is C. Such languages are referred to as *hybrid object-oriented languages* as opposed to *pure object-oriented languages* such as Smalltalk. In a hybrid object-oriented programming language, some data have predefined types (such as integer, string), while others are created from classes. C++ was developed in the early 1980s. Because in the C language the ++ operator increases the value of a variable by 1, C++'s name implies that it represents an incremental step beyond C.

A significant advantage of C++ is its appeal to established C programmers. It can be used as a stepping stone to adopting the object-oriented approach. One can use C++ to write C code: most of the valid C programs will compile under a C++ compiler written by the same company for the same environment. The other side of this equation is that many purchasers of the new compilers now available may well be using C++ in the same way in which they would use C. Using an OOPL without previous OOA and OOD activities does not generally yield the benefits expected from the object technology. In addition, there are facilities in C++ by which a skillful C programmer can access directly the class data members and therefore break encapsulation, losing thereby the advantages inherent in modularization and low coupling.

C++ extends the C *struct* construction, by adding the *class* construct. Class *member functions* perform the operations of a class, and class *data members* hold the state of the class instances.

Smalltalk/V and C++: A Comparison

C++ and Smalltalk/V have different strengths, which spring from their different backgrounds. Smalltalk/V attempts to shield its user from the characteristics of the operating system. It features weak typing, dynamic binding (determination at run time, rather than at compile time, of the object that is the receiver of a message), and an extensive development environment. C++, in contrast, is able to manipulate elements of the system at the low level provided by the C language. C++ is strongly typed, supports dynamic binding in a limited form, offers multiple inheritance, and does not include a development environment as part of its basic definition. It is not a pure object-oriented language, as is Smalltalk/V. The developer can use the object-oriented paradigm, but it is not enforced.

Two distinctions in C++'s implementation of object orientation are multiple inheritance and encapsulation. On the other hand, experience has shown that experienced COBOL programmers have a hard time adapting to the C++ discipline, while finding it much easier to learn Smalltalk [OOP93] encapsulation. Multiple inheritance allows the developer to specify that a class can inherit from more than one superclass. A resolution mechanism is supplied for occasions where the superclasses provide conflicting operations. The language has a range of ways to express various levels of information hiding. Member functions and variables may be private, or public, or have an intermediate *protected* state, which allows only the class and derived classes to have access to them. In Smalltalk/V privacy cannot be enforced, but it is not possible to make variables public and thereby break the encapsulation.

Smalltalk is usually implemented by a dynamic compiler and an interpreter. In contrast, C++ is typically implemented by a conventional compiler that compiles the C++ code directly, or by a preprocessor that converts the C++ constructs into C code that is later processed by a C compiler. Finally, C++ does not include any specific environment or class library (whereas Smalltalk/V does), although the compiler vendor may supply either. Those components can also be purchased separately from other vendors.

Knowledge-Based Systems

In order for knowledge-based, or expert, systems to be accepted at the corporate level, their development should be business as usual, not an exception. Analysts at MIS shops, not only "backroom gurus," should be able to build KBSs. The primary bottleneck in the development of expert systems applications is acquiring the knowledge. There have been many attempts to solve that bottleneck. Rule-induction systems and techniques such as case-based reasoning programs have achieved some success when handled by knowledge engineers, but not so much in the hands of end users. Repertory grids and other techniques promise some formalization of the knowledge-acquisition process, but their acceptance is not universal.

Object technology can help solve that bottleneck. In this technology objects represent real-world elements. Objects exhibit behavior and encapsulate knowledge. Object representation is well known in the field of artificial intelligence, where the more general term for knowledge representation with this technology is *semantic networks,* with its particular version called *frames.* Many knowledge-acquisition techniques address the elicitation of knowledge in terms of rules, but not many address the building of frames. Although in their inception frames were meant to represent prototypical knowledge, more and more KBS frame-based tools are implementing frames as knowledge-structure templates; that is, values in frames are not usually inherited by frame instances. A frame is therefore similar to a class in object oriented programming.[4]

Object technology has evolved outside the artificial intelligence community, but its application to KBS has the following advantages:

- Objects and frames are isomorphic.
- Object technology is starting to be accepted by the MIS community.
- There are several formal methodologies for finding object classes and methods.
- KBS tool vendors are starting to call their products *object-oriented tools*.
- Fast prototyping, emphasized in knowledge engineering, is also part of the object technology methodologies.
- The client/server computing model, native to object technology, contributes to solving the problem of distributed knowledge bases (KBs).
- Object technology promotes the reuse of software through techniques such as inheritance, aggregation, and composition, which could improve productivity when building KB applications.

We have mentioned the importance of CASE tools in an integrated, repository-based environment. The next section describes the role of CASE tools in object technology.

4.3 Object-Oriented CASE Tools

It has been observed [YOU92] that virtually all world-class software organizations are using CASE technology, but not all organizations using CASE are world-class software organizations. The importance of modeling in object technology strengthens the need for object-oriented CASE tools, which are beginning to enter the marketplace. This chapter describes the requirements for object-oriented CASE tools and recounts some actual experience with them in different stages of the application development life cycle.

---

4. Frames are groups of related facts, held in slots that are similar to object attributes. Demons, which are procedures attached to either a slot or a frame, are similar to methods. Demons, however, fire automatically at specific points in the inference process, whereas methods fire whenever they are invoked by a message [AIK92].

Requirements

Most of the available object-oriented CASE tools are rather primitive. It has been suggested [LUK92] that such tools must meet the requirements listed below in order to realize the productivity levels that can be achieved through object technology.

Basic Requirements

- Diagram-drawing support, with icons for all the notation symbols required by the different methodologies

- Icon creation and customization for new methodologies

- Facilities for symbol placement, sizing, redrawing, and alignment

- Quick editing, updating, saving, and retrieving of symbols and diagrams

- Intelligent connections (rubber-banding) between diagram elements, so that, for instance, when a class is moved in the diagram, the associations move with it, and the system automatically redraws the diagram, maintaining its intelligibility and clarity

- Large virtual drawing space with scrolling facilities and multiple window support

- Zooming capabilities

- Folding and unfolding of the system diagram at different detail levels (such as system, subsystem, and class levels)

- Layering, for displaying some layers and not others (for instance, the class, class structure, and association layers could be displayed together or independently)

Advanced Requirements

- Automatic translation between equivalent notations, given a mapping between them (assumes equivalence and the existence of an underlying conceptual representation)

- Analytical capabilities, to provide analyses of polymorphism, inheritance, and access paths

- Error and consistency checking (for instance, flagging classes without attributes and associations)

- Import and export of models from and to other applications

- Model- and class-level versioning

- Code generators: headers and structure details obtained from the class diagram, and body generation from the state and event flow diagrams

4.4   Information Modeling

One of the requirements for an ideal object-oriented CASE tool is the support of multiple interrelated models that must be kept consistent one with another (see Figure 4.4 and Appendix A, "Design Notation for Documentation"). At the top of the diagram is the application model. In the context of object technology, this is an object model with the addition of models describing the effects of events on the state of the model (such as the state diagram and the message flow diagram). If the application model was developed using information-modeling techniques, it will include an E-R model, and it could be a subset of a business-area model, which is a refinement of an enterprise model. The data model, which maps to the logical relational database tables, is most often represented by an EAR model.

The model-view-controller paradigm is a way of structuring object-oriented models. The model, view, and controller classes in this paradigm are all part of an object model, but they are different

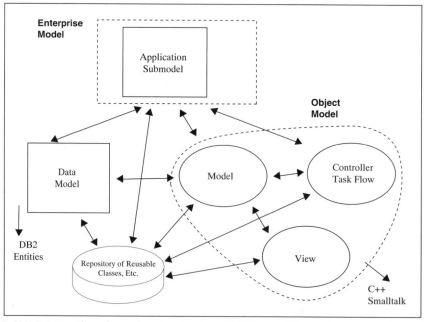

FIGURE 4.4   The ideal object-oriented CASE tool. This tool supports formal transformations among all shapes in *two* directions.

elements of that model.[5] These model definitions must be synchronized with the existing repository of classes, entities, and relations that have been derived in the analysis and design phases. In addition, all the models are related. Therefore, the information in one model should be consistent with the information in another.

Generated code can be one form of output from the various models, once sufficient work has been done. An ideal CASE tool should therefore be able to generate object-oriented programming language statements directly from the object model, provided that the methods and variables have been defined.

Working in the opposite direction, that is, going from object-oriented code to the object model, should also be possible. This is called *software reengineering*, which is conceptually easier to imagine for an object-oriented CASE tool than it is for one based on functional decomposition, because the code retains the essential structure of the models. Mapping in either direction is therefore simpler.

4.5   Object-Oriented CASE Tools: An Example

A CASE tool that supported object-oriented concepts was used to develop the Game application in this book.[6] The experience of using that tool confirmed the productivity that can be achieved with integrated models.

Requirements Definition

The starting point for the development of the Game application included two high-level objectives. These were subdivided into a number of levels, because each objective included a number of subgoals. Requirements were stated for the way in which the Game was to be produced as well as for what the end product was to do. A requirements statement was produced for the Game objective, and this was turned into a more formal problem statement. In addition, a typical scenario for the Game was produced, involving a character moving about a maze. These elements provided all the basic material to proceed. The tool captured the objective statements. The full problem definition and the scenarios were kept outside the tool as text files.

---

5. *A distinction should be made between the* model *part of the model-view-controller construct, and the* model *produced in the object-oriented analysis phase. The latter is used for designing and building the former. In addition, the user interaction needs to be modeled; therefore, the corresponding classes are also part of the object model.*

---

6. *The step-by-step development of the Game application and its corresponding code are described in Appendix B, "The Game: An Example" and Appendix C, "Smalltalk Code of the First Iteration."*

At the application-scoping stage, several decisions were made about the scope and nature of the Game application. These decisions concerned such things as the target platform, the interfaces with other environments, and the form of data the application was to handle.

Properly speaking, these considerations fall within what is called the *end-to-end design*, which at present stands outside the object-oriented development process. End-to-end design is a methodology that focuses on anticipating the issues involved in building any complex computer system. It addresses large issues such as performance, security, systems management, availability, and project risk. The methodology is used after a set of requirements has been identified and before any analysis and design work has been done. The tool used was unable to capture any of this data and the associated decisions. This was not unusual, as most other CASE tools also lack this ability.

An Entity-Relationship Model

The tool that was used had an underlying representation of objects in the form of an E-R diagram and could convert from one model to the other by command, as long as the entities represented the same real-world objects required by the application (which was not always the case). Therefore, the next step was to build an E-R model to represent the application domain. Part of this model appears in Figure 4.5. Because no general entity models were already available to draw from, the model was produced by analyzing the application requirements statements. The model was refined a number of times until it became relatively stable.

Note that the E-R methodology supported by the tool included a number of features that are not universal. For example, there is the subtype relationship, represented in the diagram by the lines connecting GameCharacter to You and OtherCharacter. This translates very conveniently—in this example, at least—to an inheritance link in the object model. This E-R model became part of the input to the object model.

An Object Model

The E-R model was transformed into an object model directly by the tool. It was then necessary to refine relationships into appropriate links and check the translation of entities into objects. For example, not all of the entities in the E-R model became objects in the object model, because the analysis covered more ground than was necessary to implement at this stage.

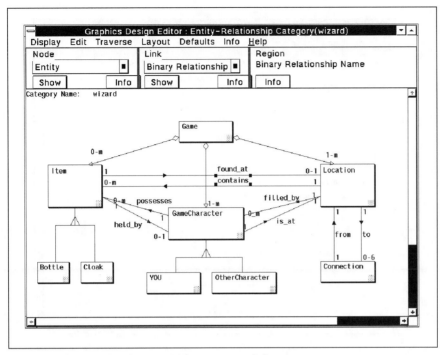

FIGURE 4.5   An E-R diagram of one part of the Game

The overall object model was developed using a number of different partial submodels (called *categories* in the tool). There was, for instance, a model that showed only the Model objects of the model-view-controller structure and a model that showed only the View objects. Figure 4.6 shows part of the Model submodel of the Game. This submodeling approach simplified the process of comprehension and manipulation. These subviews of the object model had to be consistent, because some objects could appear in more than one submodel. The tool maintained this internal consistency: the Game object in one category was always the same as the Game object in another.

A further refinement of the object model is the design of the internal structure of the objects. This activity included building methods and variables to support the links that were defined in the high-level object model. The window in Figure 4.7 shows the internals of the Item class (the tool calls this the *class structure*) with three variables (*Id, Description*, and *Size)* and six methods. This is just a sample of the complete list of Item's methods. The *listActions* method line shows, for example, reading from left to right, that it is a public method, takes no parameters, and returns aDictionary instance when invoked.

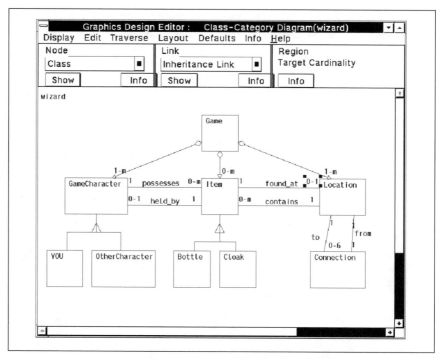

FIGURE 4.6 An object model diagram of one part of the Game

The tool itself has automatically displayed the fact that there are links between Item and Location, and Item and GameCharacter. It has derived these links from the higher-level class category diagram. (See Figure 4.6.)

A Dynamic Model

As discussed in Chapter 3, "Object-Oriented Analysis and Design," object models only provide a static representation of the application. To analyze the dynamic behavior, the methodology must be able to capture this behavior. The technique used in the tool is that of scenario modeling. This shows the flow of messages (approximately equivalent to Rumbaugh's *event flow* or Wirfs-Brock's *collaboration graphs*) between objects.

A scenario is a particular sequence of events that can occur during the operation of a system. Obviously, it is possible to produce a scenario for each and every event, but it is far more common to concentrate on certain objects and common sequences. Figure 4.8 shows the detail-level message flow that must occur between classes in order to move a character within the maze.

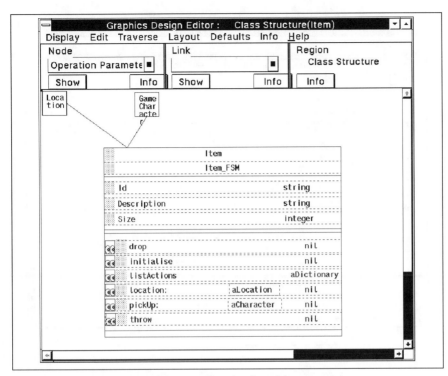

FIGURE 4.7   Examining the Item class in the object model

Users, through some function in a view window (for instance, pressing a button) indicate that they wish to go east. The view generates a message corresponding to that event, which is sent to the appropriate GameController object. The GameController passes it on as another message to the relevant character object, in this case aYou, which is an instance of the You class. The object aYou asks itself where it is. Having found out that it is in room1, it then sends the message remove to room1, an instance of the class Location. When that operation has completed, aYou finds the new location by asking room1 for it, and room1 gets that information from aConnection. aYou tells the new location, room2, to add aYou to its list of characters and finally tells itself that room2 is its new location.

The GameController is hidden from the way in which You changes to its new location. You does not know how Location handles its knowledge of the other locations that are connected to it. This encapsulation is ideal from the programming point of view, but it is important to know at various points what is happening when the state of the system changes. This dynamic model represents one such state change.

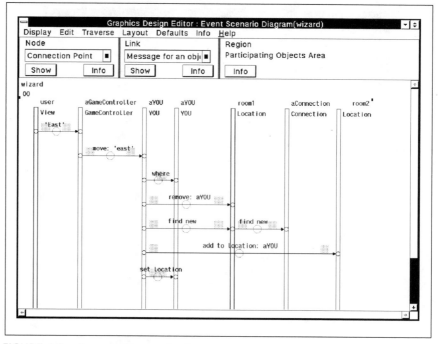

FIGURE 4.8   An event scenario diagram

The tool did not appear to emphasize or exploit these event scenarios elsewhere. The objects that appeared in them were extracted from the single repository and thus were identical in name at least with the same objects in another diagram, but nothing beyond that. The messages between objects, for example, were not linked to the methods described elsewhere in the object model. It will take some time for tools to achieve the level of integration that object-oriented concepts now allow.

From Design to Code

The tool was capable of outputting C++ code from the object model. The code was skeletal, giving the appropriate structure for the classes, variables, and methods at a basic level. Because there was no link to the event scenarios, there was no representation of what the behavior of any method might be. Thus, the code generation was only a step in the right direction, leaving all the behavior of the objects still to be coded by a programmer.

Documentation Tools

As noted in the previous sections, object-oriented CASE tools are indispensable for guarding the consistency and coherence of large projects. For small projects, or for groups that are just beginning to explore object technology, a documentation tool may be sufficient.

The dividing line between CASE tools and documentation tools is in practice very thin. There are CASE tools that produce mainly model drawings, and there are documentation tools that have certain code-generation capabilities. An ideal CASE tool should, of course, cover the complete application development life cycle and even control the changes in the implementation of an application that could contradict the analysis model. A documentation tool covers only part of the process, and manual work is necessary to transform the output of one development phase to the next. The consistency of analysis, design, and implementation is therefore also a human responsibility.

If the only objective of a documentation tool is to produce documents, then a word-processing tool might be considered. In order to document an object-oriented analysis and design activity, however, the tool must be aware of the *structure* of the information to be documented. More specifically, any object-oriented documentation tool should be able to recognize objects, classes, methods, messages, and relations between classes and help the user to organize information about them.

OOATool

This section describes an example of a documentation tool: OOATool, by Object International, Inc. This tool supports the object-oriented analysis method of Coad and Yourdon.

OOATool is the first in a series of tools that will cover the total development process as described in the OOA and OOD books by Coad and Yourdon [COA91a, b]. OOATool can be classified as a documentation tool.

All constructs in the Coad-Yourdon analysis methodology are supported in OOATool. A Coad-Yourdon OOA model consists of five layers: *subject, class-&-object, structure, attribute,* and *service.* The subject layer allows the user to group classes and objects together. The structure layer shows inheritance relationships and whole-part relations between classes. The attribute and service layers contain information about instance variables, methods, and messages.

The information for an application analysis is kept in a *model.* The representation on the screen is controlled by one or more *drawings.* For a drawing, there are many ways of tailoring the information shown on the screen, such as hiding classes or layers, or grouping classes together. Thus, it is possible to distinguish various areas of a design and hide or simplify parts of it to make it more understandable.

Additional development facilities are expected to be included in other releases of OOATool.

Figure 4.9 shows the class model for the Game, drawn with OOATool.

4.6 Non-Object-Oriented CASE Tools

It is possible to identify a number of strategies that could extract value from any existing inventory of CASE tools. However, the application of these tools is not straightforward.

The first strategy is to use existing CASE tools only for modeling the high-level enterprise and business areas. The problem with this strategy, however, is that there is no direct integration of the output of that phase with the object-oriented model, given the difference in the levels involved.

The second strategy is to use CASE tools in the absence of other tools that properly support object-oriented approaches, to provide modeling support throughout the application development life cycle. This is problematic, however, because modeling objects requires a different way of thinking about applications. Using structured analysis

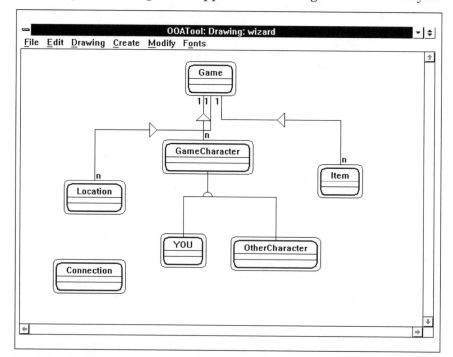

FIGURE 4.9   The Game in OOATool. The figure shows the Game, with the attribute and service layers turned off. The instance connections (1-1 relationships) between Location and Connection are therefore not visible.

CASE tools and then coding in an object-oriented programming language may simply result in procedural code in a different guise. It will be more rather than less difficult to produce good results this way.

The third strategy is to use standard structured analysis (with support from CASE tools in the form of data flow diagrams and entity-attribute-relationship diagrams) and then proceed to object-oriented design. This approach is rather awkward. One of the major advantages of object orientation is being able to use the same model or metaphor of objects throughout development, from what the user talks about to what the developer codes. This is too great an advantage to lay aside casually.

The fourth strategy is to use the CASE tools only to design the working of the internals of the objects. The system can be fully designed in terms of objects, yet their internal structure is accessed by methods that are simply functions. Design at the detailed level of these functions is similar to structured functional decomposition, and one might consider using data flow diagrams and structure charts. This does not break the object paradigm, because at this level the implementation of the features is hidden from the rest of the system. However, this approach is not realistic for many of the small methods one finds within objects.

Only the first of these strategies is acceptable in the long term. It is best to acknowledge that modeling tools are most useful in the environments for which they were designed. Therefore, once the high-level business analysis has been completed, it is better to look for tools that clearly support object orientation than to use existing, long-established CASE tools with this new approach. This is not to deny the likelihood that well-established CASE vendors will bring out new versions of their tools that support the new methodologies. Appropriate CASE support for object-oriented methodologies is starting to appear in the market.

Thus, the conclusion is a mixed one. Many of the concepts and notations made familiar by current CASE technology will live on in the new world. Object-oriented analysis and design is an evolving area, and many of those involved in its definition come from a traditional background. Moreover, some authors make explicit their desire to use familiar terms to introduce the readers to unfamiliar ideas.

New techniques, and extensions of the old, will have to be adopted, however. For any tool to be useful in object technology, it must be able to support notations that express the object-oriented concepts of objects, inheritance, and encapsulation.

4.7 Summary

- The utility of any object-oriented CASE tool should not be overemphasized for small projects, and the tool may not be cost-justified in those cases. Nevertheless, an object-oriented CASE tool is certainly a "nice to have" tool, given the amount of interrelated drawings required in object-oriented modeling.

- The real benefit is bound to make itself felt in larger projects, either with hundreds, going on to thousands, of classes, or with complex preexisting entity models. In those cases, being able to maintain a consistent model of the problem within the context of the business as a whole is a major benefit.

- Documentation of an application through its model, held and modified dynamically as the objects in the application themselves change, is of great interest. The iteration that object-oriented methodologies encourage will not happen in practice unless there is adequate CASE support.

- It is also clearly not sufficient to think of an object model only in static terms; dynamic behavior is something that an object-oriented CASE tool must be capable of representing clearly.

- The final practical requirement for an object-oriented CASE tool is that is be integrated with a development environment, making the transition from analysis to design and coding seamless.

The User Interface and Visual Programming

In this chapter we describe the issues involved in building a user interface. We also discuss the concepts and applications of visual programming tools.

5.1 The Model-View-Controller Paradigm

During the evolution from an analysis model to a design construct, it is necessary to consider not only the implementation environment but also how information will be presented to the end user, and how the end user will interact with the application. To facilitate these considerations, it is useful to partition the application architecture according to the *model-view-controller* paradigm (see Figure 5.1). The concept as defined here was formulated first for Smalltalk programming environments, but in fact it is independent of object orientation. Goldberg and Robson [GOL89] is a good reference on the subject.

The elements of the model-view-controller paradigm can be described as follows:

- Model—A representation of the application domain as an object model

- View—A specification of how aspects of a model are represented to the user

- Controller—The specification of how the user can communicate or interact with the application in order to request changes to the view, or to the underlying model

Many direct-manipulation frameworks combine the view and the controller roles, because there is a close coupling between the way in

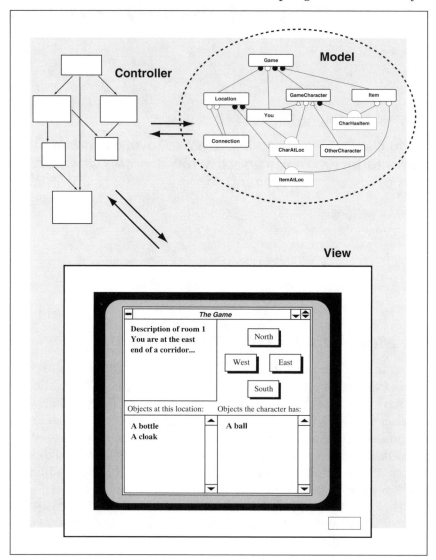

FIGURE 5.1 Model-view-controller. The model represents the static aspects of the application. The view is the way information is represented to the user. The controller represents the interaction with the user.

which the information is presented and how it is manipulated.

The example of the Game application (in Figure 5.1) shows that

- The model is the group of classes from which the basic Game objects are created: Game, GameCharacter, Item, Location, and so on.

- The controller specifies the rules for how those objects are to interact. The GameController defines what messages should be sent when there are interactions with the user.

- The user can only make changes by means of control objects represented on the screen. Those control objects are usually integrated into a view. For instance, when the user "presses" (selects) the button labeled "North," an event is generated and then picked up by the particular view that handles the direction-control buttons. The view sends a message to the GameController, which in turn sends a message to the aYou object, telling it to move.

Thus, the view can only change the state of the model through the controller. If the application requires these changes to affect display areas in the screen, a warning mechanism is established between the model and the view. The model alerts the view that changes have occurred, and the view "refreshes" the value of the variables it displays.

Views can present one underlying model in multiple ways to a user, for example, graphically and textually. Thus, in the first version of the *Game,* Items were presented to the user by means of a list. In the second version they appeared as icons in a window. Changes to the underlying model were not required to enable this (apart from defining the icon that was associated with each item).

The controller regulates and synchronizes the flow of messages between the objects. Its purpose is to ensure that the objects abide by the rules. A strong set of controller classes makes the application more procedural and easier to manage. A weak set of controller classes gives the user more freedom and is more suitable for inquiry or exploratory tasks. As in the real world, it is convenient to establish a separation of responsibilities. This strengthens the argument for designing separate classes for user activities.

5.2   The Graphical User Interface

The development of a graphical user interface (GUI) has been frequently associated in the trade press with object orientation. It is indeed true that icons, windows, and direct manipulation (drag and drop) give the user a visual representation of real-world objects that makes it easy to understand how to perform a specific task. The computing style by which users interact with the application by performing actions on objects (mainly those displayed on the screen) is called the ***object-action paradigm.***

Historically, Smalltalk was developed as a language for testing ideas about what a GUI should look like, but the development of an object-oriented interface in Smalltalk is text-based. Indeed the creation of a usable window takes just a few statements. For example, the Smalltalk expression

```
LearnWindow :=
  TextWindow
        windowLabeled: 'Learning Status'
        frame: (125 @ 125 extent 425 @ 225)
```

will create a text window with editing capabilities. It is not easy, however, to find and master the proper syntax for the numerous kinds of windows the user might want to create, including panes, subpanes, and special controls. This is a serious obstacle to increasing the productivity of the application developer. Some current estimates suggest that, in many applications, building the user interface takes as much as 75 percent of the total development effort. With adequate tools, and once a particular set of interface classes has been learned, the interface effort shrinks dramatically.

5.3 Screen Painting

One way to improve the productivity of the programmer when building user interfaces is to use a screen painter. A good example of such a screen painter, which is fully integrated with the Smalltalk/V environment, is WindowBuilder, by Objectshare, Inc. Figure 5.2 shows an example of the use of WindowBuilder to develop a version of the user interface for the Game application.

In WindowBuilder the user paints an application screen by dragging icons from the left side to the *layout pane*, the place where the window is built. When an icon is dropped on the layout pane, a new instance of a pane is drawn, which can be appropriately sized and moved. A complex window can thus be painted much faster than with Smalltalk/V alone, because it is easier to get all positions and sizes right visually than by textual description.

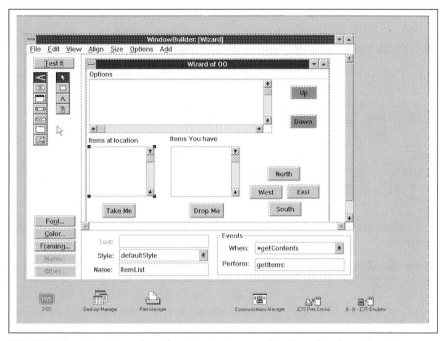

FIGURE 5.2   User interface for the Game application developed with WindowBuilder

WindowBuilder does more than just screen painting. It also generates Smalltalk/V code to open the window, and skeleton methods to respond to events such as mouse clicks. WindowBuilder can also import or export resource files. This allows applications to be prototyped in Smalltalk/V and later on built in another language, using the same (window) resources.

5.4 Visual Programming

Programming can be defined as specifying a method for doing something a computer can do in terms a computer can interpret [SHU88]. The method of traditional programming was designed primarily for efficient interpretation and execution by computers. This approach requires people trained in programming skills; it is difficult for end users to create such specifications.

Visual programming represents a real breakthrough in that situation. Facilitated by the computing power now available in desktop machines, it is based on the expressive power inherent in graphics. Visual programming has been defined as the use of meaningful graphical representations in the process of programming.

There are two main types of visual programming activities. The first type uses graphical techniques and pointing devices to provide a *visual environment* for program understanding, construction, and debugging; information retrieval and presentation; and software design and maintenance. The second type involves visual programming languages that are designed to handle visual information, support visual interaction, and allow programming with visual expressions.

In a visual environment, *showing* is the primary means of communication between humans and computers. The computer shows users what they have (in terms of data or system design), what is going on (in terms of execution states), and what to do (visual coaching). In contrast, visual programming languages *tell* the computer what to do.

Visual programming languages allow users to program with graphical expressions. A visual programming language is one that uses some visual representations (in addition to or in place of words and numbers) to accomplish what would otherwise have to be written in a traditional programming language. In a visual programming language, the language primitives (for example icons, lines, arrows, and form constructs) have well-defined syntax and semantics. The "sentences" expressed in these languages (for example, icons connected with flow paths, nodes connected by arrows) can be "parsed" and "interpreted."

Iconic programming languages are those in which icons or graphical symbols are designed to be programming language primitives. The primary objective is to teach and carry out programming concepts by pictorial representations. The "desktop metaphor" used in OS/2 2.1 is an example of such a language applied to the user interface. But the function of iconic programming languages goes beyond that of building iconic user interfaces. Such interfaces communicate with the computer only at the command-language level, whereas the intention of iconic full programming languages is to achieve graphically what the traditional programming languages can do, and therefore attract novices or end users to the world of programming by reducing the training prerequisites and presenting an attractive interface. To that end, the more declarative and less algorithmic the language is (that is, the less the programmer has to worry about variables, operations, flow of data, flow of control), the better. Object-oriented programming can certainly benefit from a technology that allows for graphical description of the definition and interaction of objects. The following section describes two tools that implement visual programming.

5.5 Digitalk PARTS

Digitalk PARTS (Parts Assembly and Reuse Tool Set) is an iconic visual programming system in which applications are constructed from prefabricated parts. Those parts can be visual (buttons, windows, and menus) and nonvisual (files, queries, and computations). The application interface is laid out by dragging and dropping the components from a palette (see Figure 5.3). The application's behavior is then created by drawing connections between the laid-out parts; that is, visual links are created. Those links "wire" the parts together to build applications without traditional programming (see Figure 5.4). The interface has the CUA '91 look and feel, and the work is done through direct manipulation.

The components that are connected to build an application can be the standard screen interface objects or application-specific parts like E-mail, databases, file systems, multimedia, and spreadsheets. OS/2 applications can be connected through dynamic data exchange (DDE).

The tools for developing an application with PARTS are the Catalog and the Workbench. The Catalog is a notebook that provides a selection of parts to use in building an application. Clicking on the Catalog allows a user to see the available categories of parts. The user drags selected parts to the Workbench, where an alignment tool provides layout-adjustment facilities.

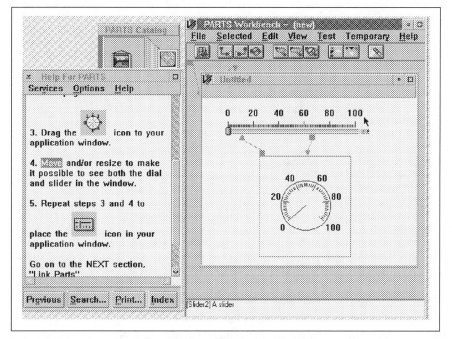

FIGURE 5.3   Creation of a user interface with PARTS

The parts can then be connected by "wiring" them one to the other. The wiring is done by drawing a line from one part to the other while holding the left mouse button down. When the mouse button is released, a pop-up menu is displayed showing all the events the source part generates and all the messages the destination part understands. Events and messages are paired up, and the wire now indicates the communication link between those parts. The completed application can now be added to the Catalog and becomes a new part to be used in future developments, saved as a file, or launched as a stand-alone .EXE program using the run-time environment of PARTS.

To modify a part that cannot be modified through direct manipulation, the user can add messages with an available scripting language that is a subset of Smalltalk/V and uses Smalltalk/V syntax. PARTS itself is a Smalltalk/V application, but it does not generate Smalltalk/V code. PARTS does not support classes and inheritance, and even though written in Smalltalk, it is not meant to interact with the Smalltalk class hierarchy. It deals with objects—parts—not with object templates. The interface to other Smalltalk programs is created by adding those programs as new parts that are accessed as functions at run time from an object library packaged as a dynamic link library (DLL). A DLL can also be built with C, COBOL, or any other language.

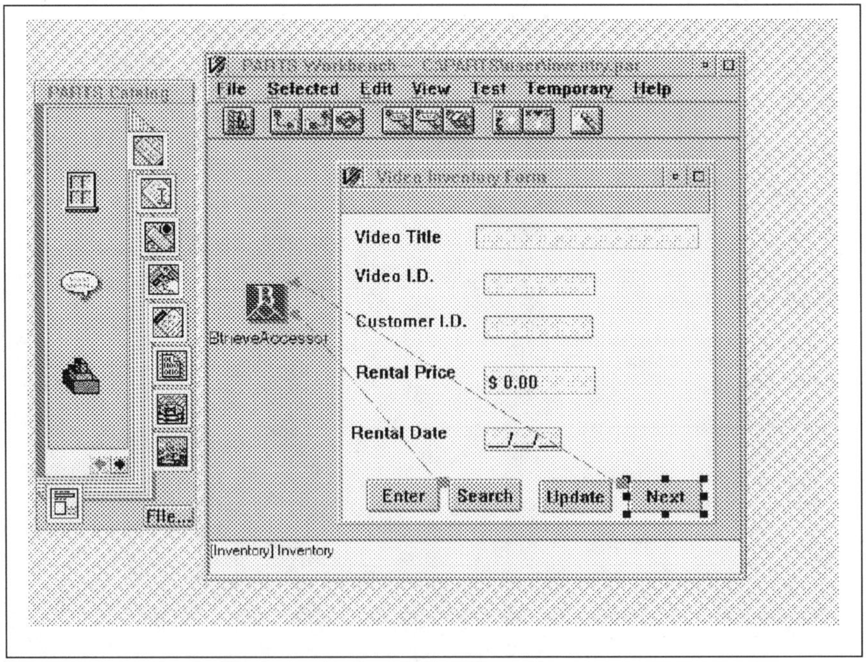

FIGURE 5.4   Development of an application with PARTS

5.6 Visual Programming Tools in the Smalltalk Environment

When used for building object-oriented applications with an object-oriented language such as Smalltalk, a visual programming tool must address the specific requirements of such an environment. The requirements can be analyzed by describing the application with the model-view-controller paradigm.

An object-oriented visual programming tool is generally used to create and modify views and the windows associated with those views. The model objects are generally the prebuilt parts available to the developer through a reference catalog. For instance, if the object-oriented application to be built is a text editor, a model object could be a saved document, and the view could be a document view (there could be many such views). Figure 5.5 shows the relation between these elements and the window.

The tool should have a screen-layout editor for defining interactive what-you-see-is-what-you-get (WYSIWYG) GUI interfaces. It should also have a view editor that allows direct manipulation (including sizing, alignment, and formatting) of views and their attributes and the possibility of connecting the constructed user interface to the object models. The developer should be able to define and work with representations of model objects corresponding to the run-time

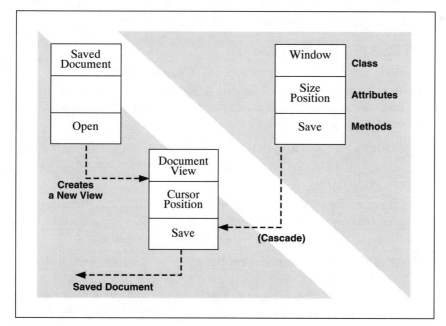

FIGURE 5.5   Objects, views, and windows

application models that the view will manipulate. These representations, or visual objects, describe the interface that application objects present at run time. The developer should be able to define directly these model objects with the visual programming tool, or use previously developed model objects.

The relationships between objects should be defined graphically, for instance, by drawing lines on the screen to connect objects. The most important types of connections required are those between events generated by some objects and actions performed by others, and view-to-model connections, indicating the relations between entry fields and model attributes.

5.7   IBM's VisualAge

VisualAge is an object-oriented visual programming application development tool that focuses on the development of client/server object-oriented business applications. It includes support for online transaction processing and decision-support applications. VisualAge enables professional developers to quickly build the client portions of the applications, complete with a graphical user interface (GUI), application logic, and local and remote resource access. VisualAge provides a pure object-oriented development environment, a set of interactive development tools, a library of prefabricated parts, and a set of highly functional components for client/server computing.

Tools and Components

Figure 5.6 highlights the variety of tools and components that VisualAge provides. Individuals in a development team use these tools and components during application analysis, design, and implementation:

- **Visual programming tool:** VisualAge provides a visual programming tool that enables the programmer to create applications nonprocedurally from existing parts.

- **Library of parts:** VisualAge's prefabricated parts include support for graphical user interfaces, and generic parts for database queries, transactions, and remote and local functions.

- **Graphical user interface support:** The GUI support included in the library of parts enables the development of applications that comply with the Common User Access (CUA) specifications with extensions to support smart entry fields, tables, and forms.

- **Client/server and communication support:** VisualAge provides comprehensive support for client/server computing over multiple protocols and programming interfaces, such as:

  - APPC (Advanced Program to Program Communications)

  - TCP/IP (Transmission Control Protocol/Internet Protocol)

  - NetBIOS (Network Basic Input Output Services)

  - CICS OS/2 External Call Interface

  - EHLLAPI (Emulator High-Level Language Application Programming Interface)

- **Relational database support:** VisualAge includes support for local and remote relational database access and queries. This support is used by VisualAge to provide visual programming parts that enable generic queries.

- **Enhanced Dynamic Link Library (DLL) support:** This feature automates the definitions that are needed to interface to a local C or COBOL DLL by building automatically the necessary objects and methods. VisualAge uses this feature to provide the generic DLL visual programming part. The DLL enhancements also provide full multithreading support.

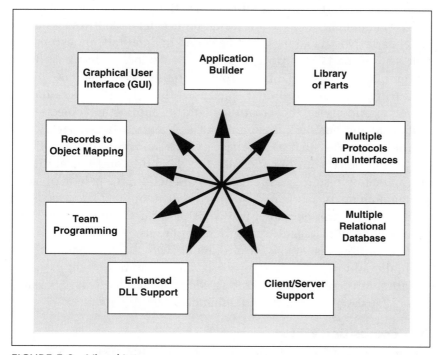

FIGURE 5.6   VisualAge

- **Team programming:** VisualAge provides comprehensive support for team programming through a central library of parts and classes in a networked development environment.

- **Configuration management:** Besides team programming, VisualAge provides support for version and release control.

VisualAge exists in two editions:

1. Personal Edition, an entry-level product for individual programmers

2. Team Edition, which provides support for team programming and configuration management

Both editions include test facilities and performance and packaging tools.

Visual Programming

Included in VisualAge is an object-oriented visual programming tool that enables the programmer to create in a graphical way true object-oriented applications composed of object-oriented classes. Using VisualAge's DLL and networking interfaces, the application can access code written in any programming language.

Under VisualAge, an application will be composed of visual parts and nonvisual parts. The visual parts are the view-controller parts of the MVC paradigm, and the nonvisual parts can be identified with the model parts. Nonvisual parts can be coded in Smalltalk or customized from generic parts that provide access to databases, business logic written in C or COBOL DLLs, or remote transaction programs.

During the development process, the visual programming technique allows for the creation of those application objects that implement the business logic and act as agents between views and external resources such as databases, DLLs, and transactions. These application objects further increase the flexibility and reusability of the application resources, and can be extracted from a palette of existing components or fabricated during the development process. Such fabricated parts can be added to VisualAge's *parts palette*, extending the available set of VisualAge services and tools.

The entire VisualAge environment was itself created using Smalltalk and the VisualAge visual programming tool. Because VisualAge was created using its own language and tools, it is possible to use VisualAge to modify and enhance VisualAge itself.

The Composition Editor

The heart of VisualAge is the Composition Editor (Figure 5.7). The developer works with this component to visually lay out the parts that make up the application, choosing the parts that perform the required functions and making connections between them, and creating composite parts made up of simpler visual and nonvisual parts. An application consists of one or more such composite parts working together.

The Composition Editor is used therefore both to construct the application logic and to design and build the user interface.

The Script Editor

The Script Editor (Figure 5.8) is a VisualAge component that helps to create and modify the Smalltalk code (called a *script)* that implements the new part's behavior. The business logic is created by writing scripts. These scripts are partially written by the system (for instance, methods to get and set the value of class attributes are created automatically by the system). The Script Editor is therefore used to implement the part behavior of the nonvisual primitive parts as represented by the actions on the part's public interface.

The Public Interface Editor

The Public Interface Editor (Figure 5.9) is where part fabricators

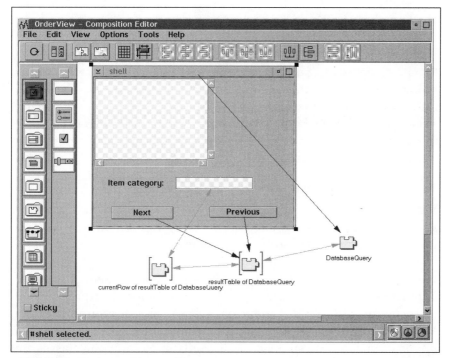

FIGURE 5.7   Composition Editor

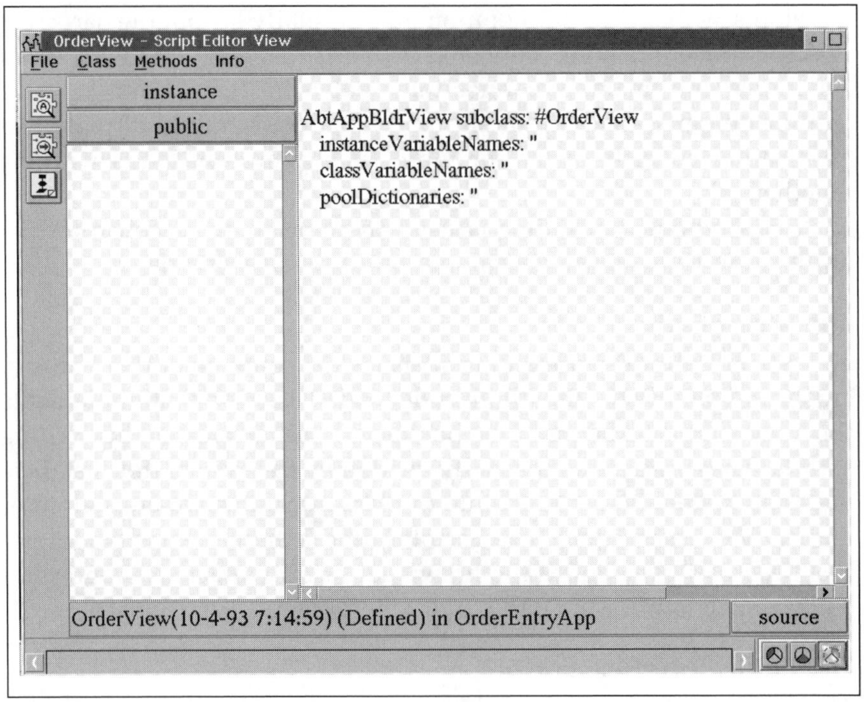

FIGURE 5.8 Script Editor

specify what characteristics and functions of a part are to be made public and, therefore, accessible to other parts. The Public Interface Editor defines a part's attributes, actions, and events. Any part that is to be a component of a composite part or an application must have a public interface, so that other parts can connect to it. The Public Interface Editor is therefore used, together with the Script Editor, when building the nonvisual primitive parts of the application. All of the prefabricated VisualAge parts have public interfaces that define the access to their functions.

Team Development Support in VisualAge

VisualAge provides an advanced environment for team programming and configuration management. The facilities provided by VisualAge for team programming support include a central repository that is located in a server on the local area network, and is used by the development team that stores the application components, enabling several programmers to share and update classes. Since multiple programmers may need to work concurrently on a class or group of classes, VisualAge allows grouping multiple classes into subsystems (called *applications).* A browsing facility is available to show the classes and

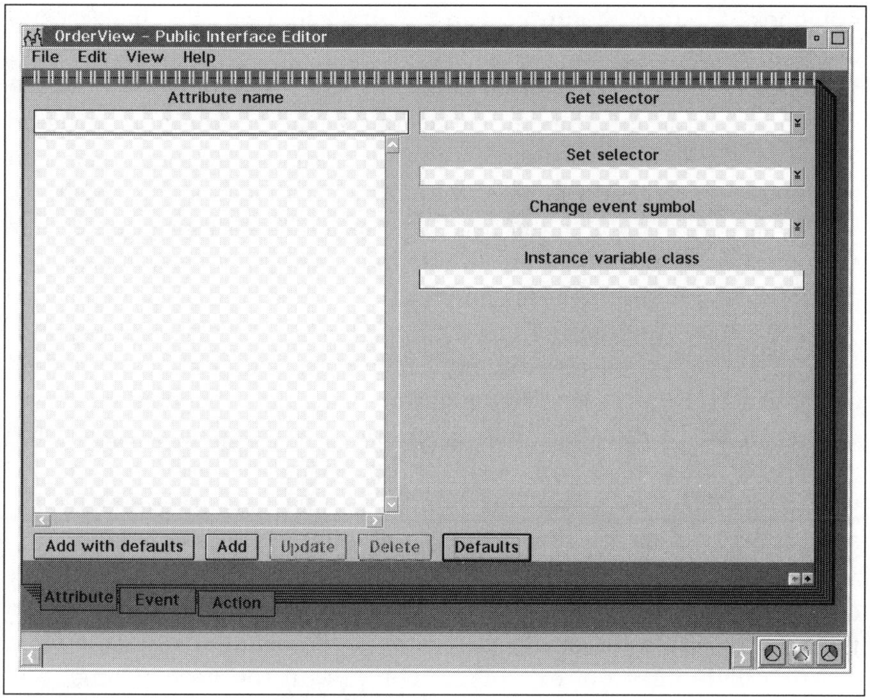

FIGURE 5.9   Public Interface Editor

the methods defined or extended within the subsystem. Within this context, VisualAge provides class and subsystem ownership identification: the owning developer has the final responsibility for the integrity of these classes and subsystems. The system provides facilities for version control and releases of classes and subsystems, plus support for prerequisites.

5.8   The Development Process with Visual Programming Tools

The introduction of visual programming tools raises questions about how those tools fit into the object-oriented development process. There are several answers to this question, depending mostly on the characteristics of the tool to be used.[1]

With Digitalk's PARTS, when the developers create new parts by using the workbench, they are creating a configuration of run-time object instances that can be stored, retrieved, and copied on demand, not a Smalltalk class. For instance, all the CUA '91 controls, such as

---

1. Although all tools will evolve and incorporate new features, the following discussion is based on the characteristics of the tools as of the moment this book was written.

notebook or slider controls, can be dragged from the palette and dropped on the screen. With IBM's VisualAge, when the developer creates a new part, the system creates a new Smalltalk class. As the developer lays out the subparts (entry fields, buttons, ordered Collections, databases, etc.) of the new part, VisualAge creates an executable description of this configuration that is stored with the class that corresponds to the part. This executable description can be thought of as an initialization routine that sets up new instances of the part. The creation of new instances of the parts built with VisualAge is achieved by sending the message *newPart* to the class corresponding to the part. The creation of new parts can be accomplished by embedding these parts inside another, using a mechanism called *composition*. At run time, the creation of the composite triggers the creation of the components. In addition, VisualAge provides a facility called *Object Factory*. This is a nonvisual part provided by the system that can create new instances of another specified class.

In PARTS, because there is no class associated with a part, it is not possible to write Smalltalk methods in the normal way. PARTS provides a certain capability for writing code using Smalltalk syntax, but this code does not execute or compile in the normal Smalltalk environment, and has a number of restrictions referring to the creation of variables, subparts, or links. In VisualAge there are no restrictions on declaring variables or writing methods for the class corresponding to the part. In addition, it is possible to add new subparts and connections.

In the VisualAge approach, the programs the user creates can be viewed in the normal manner in a regular Smalltalk environment. Browsers, and all the methods that the user writes and the variables that they declare can be seen there too. VisualAge will even optionally generate methods to recreate the executable descriptions that initialize instances of parts. This means that the VisualAge user is actually creating Smalltalk programs composed of Smalltalk classes without seeing any Smalltalk code. As a consequence, there is a smooth transition from programs developed using VisualAge to hand-written Smalltalk code.

The programs created with VisualAge are composed of a set of structured classes that support object design concepts such as model-view separation and undoable operations.

The process of building applications with PARTS has been described [COK93] as starting with the work of nonprogramming analysts, that is, people who understand the process, can lay out the screens, and can specify the functions to be performed. In the next phase, the programmers go to work writing scripts or code for the individual parts in an adequate programming environment. The programmers then create a parts catalog that lists all the component parts, which the analyst selects and wires together.

VisualAge can be used with the normal object-oriented development process model. The process starts by writing the problem specification and defining a set of use cases. The use cases are the input to the analysis prototyping phase, with the participation of the user or expert, where VisualAge is used to complete the gathering of requirements, to produce a proof of concept, to refine the use cases, and to produce the prototypes for the GUIs. The process continues along the line of the normal object development process, for instance with the aid of a CASE tool, by producing the class diagram, event traces and message diagrams, and so on. VisualAge is used here again, starting from the building of the development prototype, until the completion of the application. A mapping can be established between classes, attributes, and methods names, to VisualAge components, component attributes, and actions. The components are represented as icons, and can be linked together using visual programming techniques.

In addition, method preconditions can be mapped to a VisualAge event: an event is raised when a method is invoked, but the preconditions are not met; method postconditions can be handled in a similar manner, raising an event to indicate that the method has executed successfully, and the postconditions have been met. The GUIs developed in the application prototyping phase can be used initially for program testing; they are refined in a later stage.

VisualAge has a version that supports team development. From the perspective of object-oriented development, this requires a good definition of the subsystems that integrate the application, in order to achieve good productivity results when programming in the large.

5.9 Summary

- Building the user interface correctly is necessary to make the application usable. This activity takes time.

- Separation of the view and the model is important. A model can have different views, and is usually a stable and reusable element.

- Although the building of GUIs is time-consuming, in real business applications, the view is just the tip of the iceberg: there is a lot of work related to the development of the model part of the application.

- Visual programming tools, by helping to develop both the model and the view, are expected to play a key role in boosting the productivity of object-oriented application developers.

6

Team and Project Implementation Issues

Having the right tools is not enough to ensure the success of an application development project; knowing how to organize the human component of the project is essential. For instance, managing a project that uses a spiral or incremental development approach is different from managing a typical waterfall project.

There are other important considerations as well, which are implied by the vision of software development as a manufacturing process [TAY92] or as the production of "software integrated circuits" [COX90]. The term *manufacturing* implies that it should be possible to produce a consistent end product with high quality at a relatively low cost. In contrast, hand-crafted products, however attractive, require a greater investment of labor, are more susceptible to flaws, and cannot be mass-produced with such ease. Hand-crafting is the metaphor for today's software development; manufacturing is the metaphor for software development in the object-oriented world. Manufacturing requires different processes of management, organization, and measurement. In this chapter we describe the process of building an object-oriented application and the teamwork considerations involved in that process.

6.1 **The Structure of the Development Project**

Any project adopting object technology will have a number of new roles to consider. Where object-oriented techniques are being exploited within standard information technology organizational structures, these roles are often performed haphazardly because they lack definition, but they are generally present even if unrecognized.

The Developer

The dynamics of object-oriented development have already produced changes in the way groups of developers are working. Where more than one project is being developed using the same technology, two separate roles have tended to emerge. These roles do not mirror the established division between analysts and programmers that exists in most large information technology departments. The people who develop object-oriented solutions follow the spiral or incremental approaches outlined in Chapter 3, and are thus involved in both analysis and design. In this case, a distinction develops between those who produce generalized components, such as the abstract classes, and those who combine components to turn out applications. These two groups can be described, respectively, as *class producers* and *class consumers*, or alternatively *class constructors* and *application fabricators*.

The separation of these two functions has several advantages:

- It provides a clear division between the investment aspect of object-orientation projects and the payback, which helps in dealing with at least one of the issues raised in Section 6.4, "Metrics: Counting the Cost."

- It encourages design and code reuse by establishing a group of people who are custodians of reusable classes.

- It provides a starting point for newcomers to the field, where they can become productive quickly, fabricating applications without having to learn the intricacies of class libraries or the depths of the object-oriented programming language.

- It offers a clear focus for rapid prototyping that can use innovative products to capitalize on the investment in sound business models and objects (refer to Chapter 5, "The User Interface and Visual Programming").

A number of possible arrangements of people and organizational structures can support this two-way split. The basic procedure for turning any business requirement into an implemented system would probably be the same, however. An application fabricator would first agree with the user on a simplified version of the requirement. Then, using a library of familiar parts and asking the class constructors for any parts of which he or she is unaware, the application fabricator would use fast visual programming tools to build a component solution. This solution probably would not address all of the user's needs. The prototype might not, at this stage, query or update the real data sources or perform at a suitable level, but it would show clearly the "look and feel" of the application and provide a way to verify the accuracy of the requirements statement. Using the standard business components, the prototype would also be closer to the final application and more compatible with other applications than most prototypes can ever afford to be. In some cases, especially those with a short projected life span (which today might be programmed by the user, often with more time and effort than was ever imagined, as is usually the case, for example, with Lotus macros), the prototype may be a sufficient match, and the project would not have to go further.

Once there is an agreement on the prototype, the next step might be to refine it into an application by looking at those areas where there was no component that could handle the task. This might require the subclassing and modification of an existing class from the library or the construction of a wholly new class. There may well be whole frameworks (see Chapter 7) being built or purchased from outside to satisfy the application needs. These frameworks should be managed by the constructors, to ensure that the code developed is truly reusable and that its owner is dedicated to its maintenance beyond the current project. The final application might be a mixture of classes developed for the business by the constructors, small amounts of code developed by the application fabricator, classes bought from consultants, and classes that came with the development system or language. Far more will have been reused and modified than developed afresh, but none of this would be apparent to users, except for the speed with which their requirements were satisfied.

The Object Modeler

The role of the object modeler has a wider span of influence than equivalent roles (e.g., data modeler) in conventional projects. This is largely because object-oriented development blurs the distinction between analysis, design, and implementation (as noted in Chapter 3, "Object-Oriented Analysis and Design"). Thus, the job covers all phases of a project.

Initially, the role is to produce the object model during analysis. Afterwards it is to interpret and adapt the model to the requirements of the developers. The model also provides the project with a significant level of documentation.

The End-User Interface Designer

The days when designing an end-user interface (EUI) was merely a matter of choosing which fields to put on the screen at any one time have long gone. The majority of users are now acquainted with relatively sophisticated graphical software and expect no less from systems built for them than they would from these packages.

Any user's ability to form a good conceptual or mental model of how anything works is central to his or her ability to use it. (For an extended discussion of these ideas with many enlightening examples independent of computers, refer to [NOR91].) Fundamental to the new discipline of user interface design, then, is learning how to represent the object model in a way that makes its meaning and function transparent and, as far as possible, similar to the user model.

The responsibility of the EUI designer is to develop and support project standards for the appearance and behavior of all aspects of the user interface. A great deal of effort is involved in identifying, designing, and monitoring the implementation of consistent visual components in a way that matches the user's model. Therefore, this role is often more significant than is first imagined. It involves the interpretation of business requirements in terms of an object-oriented interface. This can encompass the design of many elements, including the following:

- The components that can appear in a window (e.g., buttons, list boxes, data fields, bitmaps)
- Permissible layout options
- Outline appearance of windows (e.g., whether resizeable)
- How the user initiates actions (e.g., by menus, mouse selections)
- Messages
- Icon design

Such elements are considered in abstract form in any number of style guides (e.g., the IBM Common User Access Design manuals). Decisions regarding what to identify as standards within a project, however, are made by the EUI designer in the context of the user's needs, and this may cause significant variation and extension. In other words, it is not sufficient to simply adopt an external standard.

Considerable thought is required to adapt it to the circumstances of the project.

The EUI designer should also be able to define formal testing procedures for the effectiveness of the interface. It is possible to measure the degree to which object-oriented user interfaces achieve targets of flexibility and intuitiveness. The designer should not assume that this will happen automatically.

Proper training and experience in user interface design is necessary to build successful applications. The training may even include principles of human psychology and graphic design. The work should not be casually left to the skills of individual designers.

The Library Supervisor

A spiral development approach increases the need to have control over the code produced during the development process. It is no longer possible to imagine a single developer working in isolation to produce code to a static set of external and internal designs. Developers return to and modify what they produce many times. During development there will be many versions of various object classes in various states of completeness.

Because object-orientation demands that many objects cooperate to achieve the business function embodied in an application, there must be a high degree of interdependence among people working on the project, whether they be (as outlined above) class constructors or application fabricators. At various stages during any project, as new classes are developed in parallel and as existing classes are refined, each developer will need to work with the latest tested versions of class libraries without putting a great deal of effort into finding and understanding those classes.

Our experience is that the design prototyping phase creates the priorities for the development of methods. Therefore, it is not possible to know far in advance the order in which classes will be developed. As soon as a small amount of function is developed, the desire is to release it to the rest of the team to test against their classes. This incremental approach demands good version control. A configuration-management system is therefore essential to the smooth running of a development of any significant size and complexity. This probably includes any project that involves iterative prototyping with the users and more than three developers.

The role of the library supervisor involves responsibility for such a system. This job is described in more detail in the context of experience with one example of a configuration-management development tool in Section 6.5, "Working with an Object-Oriented Configuration-Management Tool." Since what applies to code also holds true for documentation, models, requirements statements, and the like, the library supervisor becomes responsible for all cross-development elements that need to be change-managed.

The Reuse Architect

One of the foremost claims of object-orientation is that it encourages reuse. However, the single most unproductive aspect of coding in an object-oriented language lies in attempting to achieve this goal; that is, knowing that there is a function to be performed or an object to be defined, how is it possible to find out whether it already exists in an available class library? Experienced object-oriented developers often say that a significant amount of time (more than 50 percent) in the development of any business system is spent on becoming familiar with the capabilities of the class library. This may be an acceptable and necessary burden today, but the problem of searching for reusable functions can be expected to increase exponentially as available class libraries increase in number and breadth.

What might help is some type of specification language that can describe the general external interface of a class: what it represents and what its public methods do. Coupled with that might be a search engine, so that the functions sought could be defined. These could be combined into some form of intelligent class browser. Work is underway in this area. For example, the Object Management Group has accepted a definition of an Interface Definition Language as part of the Object Request Broker (see Chapter 9, "Industry Standards"). This definition language may provide sufficient explanation of the function and purpose of any class. Research papers offer pointers to alternative approaches, including, for instance, search engines based on text strings in methods. Tools that address these issues may soon appear on the market.

In the meantime the reuse architect has a difficult role. The most direct form of reuse will come through the exploitation of frameworks (see Section 7.3, "Frameworks: Practical Approaches to Reuse"). The reuse architect will therefore need to be closely involved in outlining the services that frameworks will provide to the project and how the use of frameworks is to be monitored. The role may be that of a frameworks designer. The reuse of business classes will require the reuse architect to deal with the object modeler to ensure that a good inheritance hierarchy is established for these classes. Beyond this, they can expect to spend time reviewing developers' output, identifying functions that can be abstracted, and encouraging generalization in coding.

6.2 Educating the Development Department

Object-oriented development clearly requires a high degree of initial investment effort. It is generally agreed that the problem is not learning the syntax of a new language, but learning the concepts and how to apply them. Although some object-oriented ideas, such as encapsulation of data and clean, uniform interfaces, are familiar to developers with good structured programming backgrounds, the use of classes and collaborating objects will not be. Initially, most programmers will write procedural code within this new environment, which assuredly will not help them exploit the benefits that object orientation confers.

Object orientation involves a paradigm shift, a new way of looking at the world. The need for adopting this new "world view" cannot be overemphasized if the promised productivity is to be achieved.

Learning an Object-Oriented Language

The debate associated with learning an object-oriented language centers on which is the best object-oriented language to learn when starting an education in object technology. The term *best* in this case may have several connotations. It may refer to the most productive language for a given task or set of tasks, or to the easiest to learn, or even to the language that provides the best mapping between the object model and its implementation.

For instance, looking at the object-oriented languages available today in the marketplace, a pure object-oriented language, such as Smalltalk/V, disallows programming outside the object-oriented structure; a hybrid language like C++ is a superset of the C language and thus allows the user to code procedurally. Both types of languages have their advocates. In the case of the pure object-oriented language, the enforcement of object-oriented concepts such as encapsulation, polymorphism, and inheritance ensures that there will be no confusion as to what object-oriented really means. In the case of a hybrid language, it is argued that there is an easier progression from a familiar paradigm to the new one.

Indeed, a pure object-oriented language is better at providing an introduction to the object-oriented concepts, especially to reuse. For that reason, Smalltalk can be considered as the better starting point. The language itself is easy to learn, and most of the time is spent learning the intricacies of the development environment and the class library. It is as suitable for people with a limited programming background as for those with many years of experience.

It may seem counter-intuitive to learn one object-oriented language when your eventual goal may be to use another, but language distinctions are not so important in this area. Again, a clear understanding of concepts is more valuable than knowledge of the intricacies of any one language. For instance, the MIS department of a large enterprise had a positive experience adding object-oriented extensions to PL/I.

Similar extensions to widespread programming languages, such as an object-oriented COBOL, will soon appear in the marketplace, easing the learning curve of the language syntax for many programmers. Remember, however, that there is no real advantage to programming in an object-oriented language without a proper, previous, object-oriented analysis and design of the application.

Building Experience

After meeting the challenge of thinking in new ways, there is still the great obstacle to reuse—knowing what there is to reuse. As things stand at present, most developers must learn the appropriate class library, which is a significant overhead. This is one reason that there is almost certain to be a clear distinction between those who have had the time to acquaint themselves thoroughly with the classes, through their own exploration, and those who will have to rely on others for guidance. Even with the advent of tools to ease the task of locating the desired functions within a class library, this situation may not change greatly.

Thus, there are at least three stages in the developer's own life cycle: novice, application fabricator, and class constructor. Other writers distinguish more roles and give them different names [LOR91]. There is, however, only one conclusion: the learning process will take an appreciable time, and it would be good to start early. Most experts advise the employment of consultants at an early stage to deliver a "jump start" and to ensure that the promise of the technology is not left unfulfilled by just delivering old-style procedural programming using structured analysis methods in a new language.

6.3 Standards and Processes Within a Project

The project should adopt a clearly defined process to ensure delivery. It is not enough to pick a programming language and recruit a development team. Even adopting a particular method may not be enough. Methods often concentrate simply on what is to be done and how to represent the outputs at the level of analysis and design, and not on how to tackle implementation in a real project environment.

Developers will need to consider the following questions:

1. Is there to be a separate prototyping phase, and will any prototype be reused (code or design)?

2. What is the change-control process to be; for example, how will changes to the model be perpetuated into code?

3. What will the error-management strategy be?

4. How much time is to be allowed for iterations in the development plan?

5. To what extent must the user agree to the design, and at what stages?

6. What approach will be adopted to code testing, and what level of quality is expected?

7. What standards will apply?

Many of these questions will be familiar to a project manager working with traditional technology, but each has a new twist within an object-oriented project. For example, how does one test a class whose instances may be used in any number of circumstances, few of which can be anticipated by the tester? In an iterative development, how do you know that a class or method is finished? What phasing will the project follow given this new form of development? (Although development is not following the waterfall approach, it is not sensible to rush into coding before planning the design to some defined extent.)

Useful standards can be found in a number of areas: those that apply to the interaction of objects and subsystems (which we discuss in Chapter 9, "Industry Standards"); user interface standards such as those outlined in a previous section; standards and guidelines at the code level to help ensure clarity about an organization's use of object technology. These should be clearly documented before beginning the development process, although they may still change as a result of experience gained during a project.

From Analysis to Design

It is essential to extract, from whatever analysis and design methodology is selected, key information on what to do in the transition to detailed design. A sample is offered here to indicate the type of issues to be addressed.

- **Naming standards.** The names for classes, methods, and attributes should match those found in the object model. Remember that the model is key documentation.

- **Publish the specifications of contracts between classes.** This should keep classes that provide services from being arbitrarily changed in ways that would affect their clients.

Detail Level of Implementation

Programming standards are still required, as they are for any structured approach to code development. No object is so well designed that it cannot be made difficult to modify by poor programming. If the models defined during the object-oriented analysis and design phase are correct and comprehensive, however, it should not be necessary to read code in order to understand a system. Therefore, less emphasis can perhaps be placed on code and more on correctness of design.

Again, a small sample of areas where guidelines are required is offered.

- **Size of methods.** Small methods that capture discrete units of function are easier to read and maintain.

- **Method documentation.** There should be comments within each method describing its purpose, creator, date of last modification, and expected input.

- **Naming.** Names of methods and variables should accurately describe what they label. A uniform pattern should be adopted. Define standard verbs for common operations. In the Game example, *add* and *remove* have been commonly used as the prefix to method names, for instance *addCharacter*.

- **Commented out code.** This should be discouraged unless it is illustrating an example of code usage or represents code awaiting the development of function elsewhere in the system.

Such recommendations on programming style lie scattered throughout the programming (and design) literature. All projects should extract their own simple rules.

6.4 Metrics: Counting the Cost

A common point in all discussions of object-oriented project management is that effort (and therefore time) are distributed differently than in a conventional project. All application development phases will be present, but in a different order and with different amounts of resources dedicated to them. Unfortunately, beyond that, it is difficult to find any substantial evidence as to the relative changes that take place. Two predictions seem reasonable: that the user requirements analysis will increase in scope as the emphasis on prototyping increases and similarly, that design will now extend over a longer period and take on yet more importance. The coding effort should decrease commensurately; exactly how much will depend on the degree of reuse achieved within the project.

Initial projects will show low productivity for three reasons:

1. There is a significant overhead associated with learning a new technology.

2. Little reuse can be made of business-specific components (since they do not yet exist.)

3. Time must be devoted to building up the business-specific components, by generalizing classes developed in the first applications.

Later projects should show a significant increase in productivity as reuse grows. This increase should be twofold. Not having to build code should save time, and the higher quality resulting from the use of standard, proven components should reduce maintenance.

As productivity rises, however, the ability to measure that productivity falls. To put it simply, it is not trivial to measure the productivity of someone who is not producing but reusing. Neither lines of code nor function points are appropriate in this situation. And how does one encourage the development of reusable code if it does not benefit the project at hand?

It is therefore important to pursue alternative metrics that could be applied to object-oriented development. Such metrics should enable the development department to measure its productivity on a particular project and also attend to the more generalized requirements necessary to reap the real benefits of the investment in object technology. From data collected about the current project, that is, size, complexity, and amount of effort already spent, it should be possible to answer questions such as, "Would it be productive to iterate around the development cycle again?" and "Does the design for class X make that class sufficiently reusable?"

However, there is at present too little properly documented experience and therefore only a limited amount of helpful guidance and (to our knowledge) no tools that implement any tested measurement methods. Useful guidelines are available [LOR93] on class design metrics, but for project metrics it is unsafe at present to generalize from the reported development projects. Too often they capture impressions rather than statistics, and come mainly from organizations in the computer software business rather than general commercial entities. Therefore, the need is stronger than usual for the development department to collect its own statistics to help in the estimation and tracking of future projects. The measurements that will be useful include:

- Ratio of key classes (often abstract classes) to peripheral classes

- Contrast in effort between developing a new class and changing an existing one

- Person-days effort per class (This will enable the development department to define effort in relation to the nature of the class, for example, whether it is a business framework class or application class, key or peripheral.)

- Effort required

- Number and duration of the major iterations in the development cycle

- Number of classes per developer

6.5 Working With an Object-Oriented Configuration-Management Tool

In this section we describe the experiences and impressions obtained from working with a configuration tool, the **ENVY**/*Developer* configuration manager. The Game application was developed using **ENVY**/*Developer*, a team programming environment for Smalltalk/V produced by Object Technology International. It was chosen as a representative example of the leading object-oriented configuration-management tools on the market today.

The Tool: ENVY/*Developer*

ENVY/*Developer* is divided into four components:

- **ENVY**/*Manager*
- **ENVY**/*Swapper*
- **ENVY**/*Stats*
- **ENVY**/*Packager*

ENVY/*Manager* is the primary component. It controls the development of Smalltalk/V applications across OS/2 PM, Microsoft Windows, DOS, and UNIX™ environments. All workstations involved in a project share the same library (or database) of source and object code, which resides on a LAN server. The developer can construct individual images using the *Manager* at any point in the development cycle, so it is possible to try things out and roll back to any point without penalty. Because all code is stored in the library files, no change or source code files are found on individual developers' workstations.

ENVY/*Manager* forces a discipline on its developers. It introduces a new structuring concept, the *application.* Applications are made up of classes that perform specific functions. They are linked to other applications, defined as *prerequisites,* which provide necessary functions that are not directly related to the problem domain (for example, window manipulation classes and basic system classes). Access to basic system classes is controlled, and it is easy to distinguish between classes that are within and outside the problem domain. A typical application might consist of five to ten classes and one to four prerequisite applications.

Applications can be considered as additional semantic constructs that allow developers to create and view a functional decomposition of the system. Standard Smalltalk/V only provides one view of how classes interrelate: the inheritance hierarchy. A hierarchy display with the Smalltalk/V class hierarchy browser indicates neither which classes cooperate to implement a system nor how they do it. Additional constructs, such as the applications, are required. Applications also provide a higher-level component for reuse than the class, because they typically provide a complete service for a requirement.

Figure 6.1 shows the elements of one application—GameApp, which is highlighted in the top left-hand window. The middle list box shows the classes in GameApp. The GameController class is highlighted, and the methods in that class are being examined. The main text pane shows the contents of the selected method, addLocDescription. As the applications browser shows, GameController is a subclass of ViewManager, but ViewManager is not a part of the application, and therefore ENVY/Developer will not allow the selection of this class.

Both classes and applications have *versions,* which are immutable snapshots taken at a particular point in time. From a version it is possible to make a new *edition* on which to work, uniquely identified by

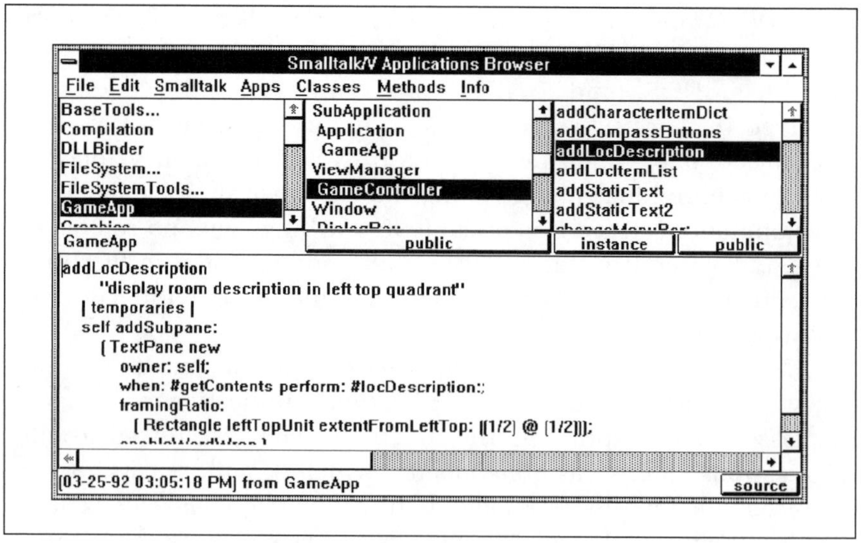

FIGURE 6.1   An example of the applications browser

a time stamp. When work has been completed on that edition, it usually becomes a new version, which will be released to the rest of the development community. Any developer can create a new edition of a class, but only the *owner* of the class or application can release the new class version. For example, a developer might decide that a particular class needs a new method. He or she would take the most current version, make a new edition, and add the method. After testing the class, he or she would submit it to the owner, who is responsible for making a version (that is, accepting the changes) and releasing it. The development environment is thus flexible enough to support the rapid prototyping mode of many Smalltalk developers, yet it still provides sufficient control over changes to the software. Indeed such a scheme of ownership is very conducive to long-term commitment to one's code. With code development goes responsibility.

Using an editions browser, it is always possible to see or load additional versions or editions that differ from the current version. Because all code is stored in a shared library, all modifications are available immediately to all developers. However, a developer will typically use only released classes and applications unless collaborating closely with another team member. Thus, a developer can load a team member's temporary fixes, try them out, and then unload them after a test even if the fixes have not been released. Having versions with explicit releases also makes it difficult to produce changes that affect the stability of the overall system without its being noticed and traced to a particular instance of some code. Figure 6.2 shows the various editions of the class GameController. The same method, *adLocDescription,* as in Figure 6.1 is being examined, but this time it is from version 1.4 of the class, rather than the most recent version, 2.0, indicated by an asterisk in the list.

Since all code is immediately compiled and available in the library, and developers maintain their images at exactly the level they want, there is no need to export code. Neither is there a requirement for a "build and integrate" step. In some sense, all images can be viewed as continuously built and integrated.

ENVY/*Manager* not only stores source code in its libraries, but also stores the object code generated by the Smalltalk/V compiler. This allows software components to be linked to the image when loaded, rather than recompiled. This mechanism improves speed two to five times when loading an application into an image, as compared to the file-in approach.

Loading components into a developer's image is an atomic transaction. Either the entire load succeeds, or the entire load fails, and the image is left untouched. This means that is not possible for a Smalltalk/V image to get "hung" in an intermediate state when a large file-in breaks in the middle.

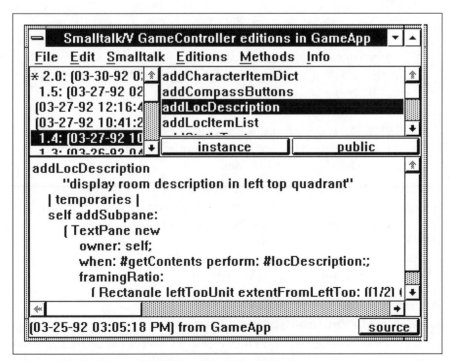

Figure 6.2   An example of the editions browser

ENVY/*Developer* provides an additional construct called a *configuration map*, which allows developers to group and manage collections of applications. This is the level that corresponds to what developers normally think of as a complete application.

As might be expected with an object-oriented configuration-management tool, **ENVY**/*Developer* is not monolithic; rather, a number of objects provide useful integrated function. One can regard **ENVY**/*Developer* as a set of tools to which one might add one's own. The **ENVY**/*Developer* user interface reinforces this impression, because it consists of a number of browsers for code, classes, applications, configurations, and the like. All this adds up to a development environment with a great deal more flexibility than one gets from the single class browser presented with Smalltalk/V. However, the interface appears more complicated than it really needs to be. Familiarity is achieved relatively quickly, but with some effort.

The other components of **ENVY**/*Developer* can be described as follows:

- **ENVY**/*Swapper* is a high-speed storage and retrieval mechanism for objects. It also allows objects to be transferred between different images.

- **ENVY**/*Stats* is a performance-measuring package within the **ENVY**/*Developer* system. **ENVY**/*Stats* can be used to provide a sampling of the code as it runs. The statistics tell what methods are run most frequently and how much time is spent on each method, as well as the aggregate time for that method and its children. It works best when used with long-running applications.

- **ENVY**/*Packager* provides a way of packaging a run-time system for delivering the executable code developed within the **ENVY**/*Developer* environment.

ENVY/*Developer* takes the complete Smalltalk/V base code and packages it into applications: Kernel, FileSystem, and so forth. It also has fixed some bugs in the underlying Smalltalk/V classes. Because **ENVY**/*Developer* saves the results of method compilations and class definitions, it has modified the base Smalltalk/V system somewhat. The changes do not appear to be particularly extensive.

A Comparison with Other Configuration-Management Tools

ENVY/*Developer* has several characteristics that set it apart from the general run of non-object-oriented configuration-management tools.

First, it is closely integrated with the development environment of its host language—that is, it replaces the standard class hierarchy browser interface to Smalltalk/V PM with browsers of its own. Effectively, one is working with **ENVY** rather than Smalltalk/V. Second, it is highly oriented toward group development. All users share the central development repository on the LAN and therefore have access to all changes (if appropriate). This is in contrast to the commonly used "check-in/check-out" access mechanism, which provides a far more tenuous and nonconcurrent connection between individual developers. Third, it operates at the level of classes and methods, building them up into "applications" that are much smaller than what we usually consider as an application.

Existing tools that are oriented toward procedural languages (such as COBOL or C) and text are not suitable for the manipulation of object-oriented code. Inheritance of state and behavior produce a complex set of interdependencies among individual classes, so classes cannot be handled as if they were independent code modules. Control must also be exercised at a far more atomic level than application or even class: in some aspects it must reach down to the smallest unit of compilable code, the method.

In addition, in the case of Smalltalk/V, the *image* (that is, all the compiled code for classes, their methods, and their variables) is held indivisibly in a small number of large files—the V.EXE file, and associated DLLs. The source code and a log of changes are two additional large files. These elements cannot be shared; each developer must have a copy. With plain Smalltalk/V, as shipped by Digitalk, the only way to perform team programming is for each programmer to have a copy of a common image file and then to file source code in and out between team members. This distribution and management of source code is a time-consuming and error-prone process.

A number of simple solutions to the problems inherent in this approach have been adopted that arrange Smalltalk classes in some form of *package.* These packages can then be transferred between developers and provide a simpler unit of code management. Version control can be included in package management. **ENVY**/*Developer* is an example of a more sophisticated form of configuration-management tool in which version control is more fully integrated, and team- and project-wide developments are properly supported. The additional complexity means, however, that a balanced judgment is required regarding the extent to which a project can benefit from its sophistication.

The Advantages and Disadvantages
of Such a Library Manager

The most immediate benefit of a library manager will be clear when a developer's image crashes just after a significant amount of work. Recovering one's work from a combination of an old Smalltalk image plus the changes log is neither quick nor infallible. The teams will see an immediate, tangible advantage in being able to share code easily among their development staff. The project as a whole will benefit from the ability to maintain separate working or development versions of the whole application concurrently: it becomes simple to distinguish between code under development and code that has been completed.

The disadvantages include the imposition of an administrative overhead and the performance deterioration associated with a distributed library manager. In addition, the project faces the risks of losing the LAN services. Developers may no longer be exposed to possible breakdown of their own systems, but this is balanced by their dependence on the availability of the LAN and the server on which the library manager resides. The importance of a high-availability LAN is increased because an interruption to service may prevent all developers from doing any project work.

Library supervisors take on a significant amount of new responsibility. They must decide what strategy to adopt with regard to the arrangement of libraries and how to mirror the project organization in the structure of applications, as well as attend to the day-to-day work of versioning applications. Education on the mechanics of the library manager would be a general requirement for all developers. Consultancy to validate the project approach would also benefit the library supervisor.

6.6 Summary

The change from hand-built to manufactured software products will not be achieved overnight. In the near future, a significant degree of opinion and personal involvement will still be necessary in the development of any but the simplest computer-based systems. This should not be feared, but it should be managed.

The following are simply guidelines for what to expect:

- Spiral development with an emphasis on prototyping should ensure that early results from projects are seen.

- It is reasonable to expect relatively slow initial progress in completing the first few projects. The learning curve is unlike that for learning a new programming language. Reuse cannot manifest its advantages immediately.

- The new technology does scale up to team development, but an appropriate tool is required to support this.

- Productivity cannot be measured easily. There appears to be no substitute for building up personal experience.

- Sometimes it may be necessary to harness the enthusiasm of the programming team, but the people involved in the project must be properly trained to take advantage of the technology.

- It will be necessary to change the structure of the project organization to accommodate new roles.

- A library and configuration management tool is key for the success of a team development effort. **ENVY**/*Developer* provides a reasonably complete development facility. It is a team development tool that is generally cost-effective in a project that involves programming by medium to large development teams.

- Although strongly integrated with the Smalltalk/V product, **ENVY**/*Developer* provides the sort of functions that one might expect in any object-oriented development environment—facilities for version control, history management, and code sharing. The same conclusions reached as to the usefulness of this product should apply for any good configuration-management tool used by a team developing in C++, CLOS, or any other object-oriented language.

7

Reuse

Two of the most important ways to improve productivity in application development with object technology are to write object-oriented code that can be reused and to ensure that such code is actually reused. It may also be possible to reuse code that was written before object technology became available. Therefore, reusable code can appear in two forms: object-oriented code and non-object-oriented code. Object-oriented code is available in the form of class libraries and frameworks (as discussed in Section 7.3, "Frameworks: Practical Approaches to Reuse"). Non-object-oriented code (be it procedural or declarative) reflects how applications have been developed historically.

Legacy code is the name given to existing modules in a language such as COBOL that must be integrated into an object-oriented environment. The following are examples of legacy code:

- CICS COBOL code developed and running on an MVS™ mainframe against a DB2 database

- C program modules

- Lotus™ macros written to drive 1-2-3 spreadsheets on PCDOS workstations

These examples obviously have different characteristics, but it is possible to consider just two basic strategies for bringing all this legacy code into the object-oriented world.

7.1 Client/Server Computing

The client/server computing model establishes a distinct separation between pieces of code (modules, programs, functions) that request a service and those that fulfill that request. The server is often thought of as the data provider, and the client as the consumer who presents the data to the user. A server has different characteristics than a client. Programming logic is more often found in the client than the server. For example, the client is most likely to be optimized for response to the user interface, whereas a server's first responsibility might be to the integrity of the data that it guards.

Although the client/server approach can be implemented in any environment, it is at present most commonly exploited across unlike systems. One example would be a client programming on a windowing workstation accessing workgroup data that is held on a group machine on a local area network. This group machine is not simply a passive repository for data; rather, it actively responds to requests, deciding which to satisfy and how. Another example is that of a host application that has been given a workstation front end. (For a more extensive discussion of client/server computing, see [TKA91], [POL92]).

These distinctions between client and server are not so obvious in the object-oriented world, where most objects perform both roles. However, the client/server duality can be a useful concept when it comes to integrating existing code with an object-oriented system. For example, the CICS COBOL application has the characteristics of both client and server, but some of the transactions that compose it may focus more on data manipulation than on the user. Being based in a transaction system, the server characteristics—integrity, ease of recovery, multiprocessing support—are all present. Thus, parts of this application are potential candidates for the role of a server. How simple it will be to convert these modules from an integrated application to a server will depend on the degree of separation that already exists between the user interface and data access logic in the code. The integration of this code with an object-oriented system is achieved across the client-server interface. Therefore, legacy code can be used by transforming it into servers that are accessed by object-oriented systems acting as clients (see Figure 7.1).

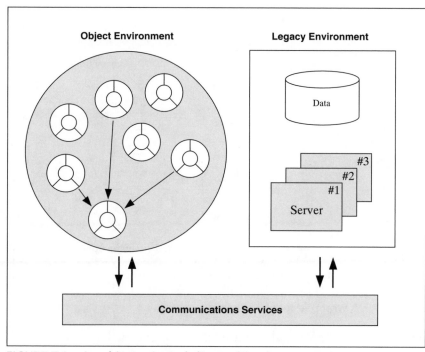

FIGURE 7.1   An object-oriented client with a legacy server

In Figure 7.1, objects use legacy code through a communications interface. The communication protocol is supported explicitly by one of the objects, which acts as the interface to the outside world. An example of this technique can be seen in the subsection entitled "Working with a Technical Framework" in Section 7.3. In the figure, the legacy code has been converted into a number of server transactions. The two environments shown in the diagram could be entirely separate, residing on physically remote machines, or the same architecture could apply within the same system.

7.2   Wrappers

The client/server architecture described above is merely a specific (and generally understood) case of hiding one environment from another to achieve a measure of seamlessness. The generic name for the technique in the object-oriented world is *wrapping* (or wrappering). The essentials of this technique involve conceptually putting a *wrapper* (an object-oriented interface) around the legacy code, thus making it appear as simply another object among many. The wrapper makes the legacy code segment behave like an object, interchanging

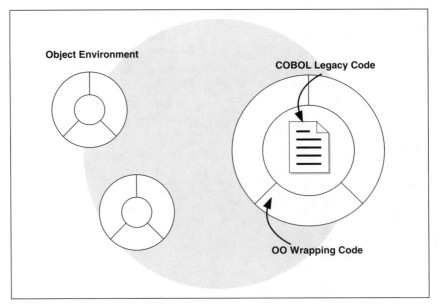

FIGURE 7.2   A wrapped legacy program

messages with its peers (see Figure 7.2). As far as the legacy code itself is concerned, nothing has changed: it continues to function as it did before. It is unaware that its only contact with the outside world is through the wrapper.

Note that the legacy procedure is only conceptually contained within the wrapping—the code itself (C, COBOL, Pascal, or whatever) is not "within" the object. It is simply that the only access to the legacy code is through the wrapping methods, just as the only access to an object's variables is through its methods. Encapsulation is complete.

If a whole program is wrapped, the effect is much like the client/server picture in Figure 7.1. There is the alternative, however, of wrapping parts of an application, converting functions and subroutines into independent (object) components, each wrapped separately, that is, each with its own message interface. Decomposing legacy code may prove to be a benefit in the long term, because the resulting objects may be reusable if the legacy code with its wrapper can be made part of a normal class hierarchy.

It is unlikely that one would ever reuse a whole COBOL program: it would be both too specific and too large to make a good object. Wrapping is applied to programs like these to ease migration to a complete object-oriented environment. First the wrapper is produced, and then, under the wrapping, the legacy code is migrated piece by piece. Alternatively, one can consider wrapping legacy programs that are not going to be changed, either because they have suffered from the maintenance warp and are no longer comprehensible or because there is no perceived benefit in migrating them. The result is that a system can look entirely object-oriented to the developer and ultimately to the user without the need for a full-scale conversion, a process that few development organizations would happily contemplate.

This is not to say that there is no cost associated with the process. Code does have to be written, and interfacing an object-oriented programming language to some third-generation structured language is not altogether straightforward. A C program running on a workstation presents few difficulties. A Lotus macro, however, represents more of a challenge, because it cannot be divorced from its environment, the 1-2-3 program. Thus, there will be some inhibitors for a while to the concept of a homogeneous system where all legacy code is entirely hidden by wrappers. The wrapper technology provides an important bridge, however, that enables migrations to object-orientation that would not be possible otherwise.

7.3 Frameworks: Practical Approaches to Reuse

In this section we describe the reuse constructs called *frameworks* and discuss their use for productive application development. Libraries of related classes intended for reuse that fall within a particular domain, for example, the domains of communications, graphics, bank accounts, or maze games, are termed *frameworks.*

It is the function of a framework to present a simple interface to the application developer for a single service or set of services, and to do this in a reliable and efficient manner. Developers might invoke the service by messages sent from their classes. Alternatively, developers might define their classes as subclasses of the framework and thereby inherit behavior and gain access to the services in that fashion. Either approach could be taken without understanding any of the complexities of the framework's implementation, with confidence that whatever is done will be consistent with what other developers in the project have done.

If frameworks are used effectively, they significantly improve productivity by keeping developers focused on the business issues rather than technical infrastructure. They also prevent common code problems from being tackled differently by each developer. Thus, a high degree of consistency can be achieved within any project and between projects.

Many companies achieve their most significant levels of reuse by exploiting frameworks. This is because reusing code within a framework can be made systematic: as with a common function, the use of a framework can be enforced. Ensuring reuse of individual components that are not frameworks or parts of a framework is far more problematical.

Realizing the potential benefits of object technology relies to a great extent on the commercial availability of frameworks across a wide range of domains. It is not in the interest of enterprises to develop their own frameworks for common requirements, for example, communications classes. This would be equivalent to deciding today to write one's own terminal interface protocol. Instead, attention within the enterprise is focused on developing the business classes, those elements that make that organization unique and help it to attain its goals.

So, where might one expect frameworks to come from, and what form might they take? In practice a framework consists of a mixture of concrete classes (off-the-shelf components) and abstract classes, which must be further refined to support a particular application or subsystem [DEN91b].[1]

At present, commercially marketed frameworks are regrettably limited to only a few areas. In particular, there is the danger that frameworks will be forever linked in people's minds to GUIs, as exemplified by MacApp™ from Apple, CommonView™ by Glockenspiel, ObjectWindows™ from Borland, and so on. As Tom Love expresses it, "We have enough string classes, collection classes, and menu classes now. [Developers should] move on to something challenging that other people do not want to build themselves [LOV92]."

Types of Frameworks

The categorization of frameworks that follows is intended to make the role of any particular one easier to understand. Current frameworks usually tend to cover a lot of ground, in order to be generally useful in a variety of circumstances. Therefore, a particular framework may not necessarily be identifiable as belonging to one, and only one, category. As the framework concept achieves greater acceptance, however, there will probably be a greater tendency toward specialization.

---

1. *Concrete classes are classes that represent real-world objects and may therefore have instances. Abstract classes are classes that describe more general concepts and have no instances. A class can be a subclass of (that is, inherit from) an abstract class or another concrete class.*

Technical Frameworks

A *technical framework* (our definition) is one that addresses basic system elements: its classes define internal computer objects or system interfaces. Such objects might be concerned with data types, such as strings, sets, and numbers, or communications protocols, or database interfaces, or how windows appear on screens. As such, a technical framework will most often be used as the basis for other frameworks.

A number of frameworks of this type can be discerned in the Smalltalk/V class library. For example, the framework of Collections contains a hierarchy of classes such as Set, Dictionary and Ordered Collection. The framework of Window Components contains classes such as SubPane, Window and ListBox. Without technical frameworks to support the chosen programming language, a significant amount of additional effort would be required to get started.

A development project of any significant size might wish to develop new or extend existing technical frameworks. For instance, one might extend the way in which collections are manipulated, or add a new visual control to the window components. In general, however, technical frameworks are increasingly complete and well designed.

Industry Frameworks

Industry frameworks follow naturally from the enterprise models that have appeared for various industries. Within IBM, architectures for the finance, insurance, utilities, retail, and other industries have been defined. One component of these architectures is an E-R model for the industry, which comprises (at a very high level) entities describing the major things a business deals with. Outside IBM, consultants are using similar architectures as a way of measuring the functional spread of a particular company and how that company addresses its markets. Again, E-R models are fundamental components of these architectures.

Still to come is the subsequent step of moving from industry analysis to designing for the industry; that is, turning the E-R models into object models and then designing frameworks based on the models. This is only realistic within the context of object technology, which has the built-in ability to take the generic industry model and extend it by subclassing to achieve a model compatible with any particular enterprise's interests. Taking one example, a framework for the utilities industry might provide classes representing customer, account, delivered service, meter reading, and so on. If based upon sound business modeling, those classes should be easily adaptable both from one enterprise to another and also within the same enterprise as it changes its business profile (for example moving the emphasis from distribution to supply).

Frameworks specific to an industry segment promise the most tangible of benefits to the business that exploits them effectively. For example, frameworks that have been written for the front-office part of the wholesale finance industry allow the computing support for new financial instruments to be created within hours rather than weeks.

Application Frameworks

An *application framework* is designed to support programming for a particular category of business problem, rather than a particular business area. It provides generic function that can be tailored for use across many workgroups.

Utilities often fall within this category. Good examples would be a graphing tool or a calendar. Graphs are used to express information succinctly and with immediate impact across a wide range of business sectors and within many forms of Information Technology application in those sectors. A good graphing framework would contain classes able to support several ways of displaying, selecting, and manipulating the underlying information. Similarly a calendar, with the function to retrieve and display information related to dates or periods, is useful across a wide range of fields. A comparable framework here might support some of the characteristics of a diary, reminder facilities, swift date selection and calculation, and calendars organizable by differing cycles (e.g., business financial periods). The user of either of these frameworks would probably need no more than a portion of the functions offered. Because they are using a framework of classes and not a monolithic application, they are free to take what is useful and discard the rest with no adverse impact on their work (assuming that the framework is properly designed).

An application framework may be used with little modification, but it may also be seen as a starting point for new function. Thus, the Game example used as illustration in this book could be considered as the basis for an application framework. The Game class and its associated classes (GameCharacter, Item, Location, etc.) would, when made suitably generic, provide the basis for many different computer games. A new game, of whatever type, would then be capable of saving and restoring its format, working with characters, and navigating around locations without any extra effort on the part of the programmer.

The Design of Frameworks

Because it is difficult to make the generalizations required for a good framework, one cannot expect to design long-lived frameworks when first learning to build object-oriented software. It is more important to become comfortable with and learn how to do object-oriented design first. Practitioners of the field point out that:

> the framework must be designed with every posssible application or subsystem in the mind of the designer concurrenlty . . . [which is] beyond the abilities of even the best designers. . . . Although a well-designed framework can minimize the need for re-design over time, it usually takes several iterations before the design becomes relatively stable [DEN91b].

Framework design is inherently iterative; a framework evolves over time. The domain of a framework often needs to be broadened during its lifetime because new uses are identified as it is used and reused by different classes of people. The graphing tool takes on activity scheduling as a form of related graphical display; the calendar acquires the behavior of a diary.

The internal and external designs of any framework are quite distinct. The external interface is what the consumer of a framework sees. It specifies the functions that the framework embodies, the messages that can be sent to framework objects, the classes in the framework that can be subclassed. The internal design of a framework is hidden from the consumer—abstract classes, and private messages, for example.

The external interface to a graphing framework might, for instance, consist in part of a specification of the following two classes,

1. DataItem, which stores graph data

2. BarGraph, the definition of one format for how graph data is to be displayed and the messages that can be sent to them.

BarGraph might include such examples as

- *displayKeys:*   the location of the graph keys
- *displayTickMarks:*   whether to display tick marks
- *displayTitle:*   the location of the graph title

The significance of the distinction between internal and external designs becomes clear when one considers how a framework is used. Every time a new version of a framework is released, applications that interact with it may need, at least, recompilation of their classes.

Often, they must be changed more radically in order to work with the new version. Thus, one cannot expect to build applications based upon frameworks that are being developed at the same time. Work is underway, however, in the following two areas:

- Investigating ways to minimize the impact on subclasses when superclasses change.

- Overcoming the need to change or recompile application classes when the framework with which they collaborate changes. For instance, the System Object Model provides a solution for the particular environment of OS/2, where the application classes are isolated from changes made to classes that belong in the operating system.

The ability of frameworks to deliver reusable software of high quality has already been proven in several specialized areas. The number of organizations offering frameworks in various categories could increase significantly, but without exploiting properly the reuse capability the frameworks provide, these efforts will remain limited in scope and potential benefit. The emergence of environments that support reusability and evolutionary change will further the advancement of frameworks.

Investing in Frameworks

Frameworks represent a change of emphasis for application development—from "make" to "buy." The initial inclination might be to resist purchasing a framework: they are often quite expensive in relation to compiler technology. Frameworks are, however, the most important investments that any enterprise is likely to make in its object-oriented environment.

Today, an enterprise that buys a third- or fourth-generation language rarely expects to buy additional components. In any case, there are generally only a few libraries or model applications available from sources other than the language vendor. The result is a tendency to think of the language as complete in itself, requiring only development tools (editors, debuggers, and the like) to make it productive. In contrast, no object-oriented development environment is complete without classes to reuse: greater productivity will stem from components like these than from any number of tools.

Any project that is based upon object technology and aims to deliver within the normal constraints of an information technology project (that is, having to provide a practical solution to a business problem, within budget, on time, and with high quality) should carefully consider the potential use of frameworks. Technical and application frameworks should be candidates for purchase rather than development (although it may be difficult to find what one desires). It is still reasonable, however, to expect some in-house development in these areas. One should also anticipate currently having to construct as part of the project the frameworks needed to support one's own particular industry.

Because good frameworks may be crucial to the success of any project, they should be developed by the most experienced staff. Those people need not only experience in the particular object technology being employed, but also with the interfaces between it and the environment within which it is operating.

Frameworks should be built early in the life of the project. The aim should be to have a stable, usable framework before other

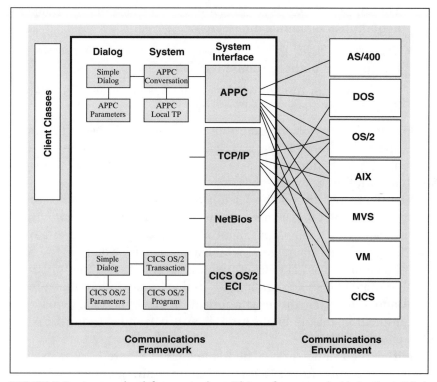

FIGURE 7.3   Layered subframeworks within a framework. Note that this is a partial representation of all the classes in the framework.

2. *The general structure of the framework should be understandable to every reader. However, since this is a real-life example, it uses existing commercial software products, such as IBM's CICS (Customer Information Control System, a transaction-oriented teleprocessing monitor) and APPC (Advanced Program-to-Program Communications) and refers to some of their characteristic parameters, the description of which exceeds the scope of this book. The reader in an MIS environment that uses IBM operating systems will appreciate the details. The reader who is not familiar with such an environment may skip the product references altogether*

developers begin to base their work on the function it provides. This does not exclude the possibility of later iterations around framework development, but these should be limited as far as possible to the internals of the framework or to extensions (not changes) to the externals.

Working with a Technical Framework

In this section we review a specialized technical framework to demonstrate how its functions are made accessible. The framework considered here is a client/server computing framework for communications.[2]

Structure of the Framework   A framework often consists of different subframework layers. The framework shown in Figure 7.3 has dialog, system, and system interface layers, representing different levels of isolation from the mechanics of the communications interfaces:

- The top, or dialog, layer provides an interface that is independent of the communications protocol.

- The system layer provides low-level support for access to the full function of the system interfaces.

- Classes within the bottom layer, the system interface, interact directly with the external systems.

For the majority of programming needs, it should be sufficient to know the top (dialog) layer. Access to the underlying interfaces is available through the other layers as required by experts who are familiar with the protocols.

The client classes on the far left of Figure 7.3 represent classes that a development department would write on top of this communications framework. The department might wish to introduce its own generic application framework, which abstracts, for example, the concept of a Client class. This Client would be able to use the functions of either the APPC dialog or the CICS dialog (or any other dialog-level class) and hide from the user application the type of client-server communication that is being used at any particular time (if that is what is required).

Exploiting the Framework   The framework of Figure 7.3 was used to extract information from a COBOL program running under CICS OS/2 and send it to the Game application. The COBOL program was built as a server, written originally with an entirely different front end. The server, however, was completely unaware of the nature of its client and therefore did not care whether it was written in Smalltalk/V or some other language.

The program is passed a key value through its COMMAREA on initialization. It then reads a VSAM file based on that key and places the record it retrieves back in the COMMAREA. The key in our case was a name, and the record returned contained details of full name, unique number, address, and the like.

It proved easy to use the framework to achieve the results required. As the diagram in Figure 7.3 indicates, the two top-level classes for the CICS OS/2 part of the communications framework were a simple dialog and a parameters class, called respectively CICSOS2SimpleDialog and CICSOS2ConnectionSpec. Thus, the primary function of any application that uses this framework is to create an instance of each. CICSOS2ConnectionSpec is set to contain the CICS program name, logon, and password. CICSOS2SimpleDialog is created with that connection specification as a parameter and also has an input and an output record specified. The process of initiating the server transaction is performed by a message, *doit,* sent to the Dialog, which returns either an error or the relevant record. Data must then be extracted from the record (by field name if this is available and the output record structure has been set up appropriately).

The fact that the framework uses other classes in the sublayers to perform the connection to CICS and translate the record structures into something that can be recognized by OS/2 is completely hidden. Thus, encapsulation of a complex external interface is achieved well. It proved far easier to expend the effort on exploring this framework than to write classes to perform equivalent function.

7.4 Summary

Some important points became clear through the process of using the framework:

- Reuse is the main argument behind the productivity enhancements promised by object technology.

- Reuse can be achieved in many ways. The use of frameworks has the highest potential to achieve productive reuse.

- A framework must not just encapsulate function; it must clearly hide complexity. If too much knowledge of the underlying technology is exposed through the framework—the fact of its being based upon a transaction system, for example—the encapsulation has been effectively broken. The framework used in this study hid this knowledge at the programming level, but not when it came to the interpretation of errors.

- Documentation is key. Even though using the framework eventually proved to be as easy as the developers thought, unfortunately they had not provided documentation as to how their classes interacted (as opposed to what they were). Thus, the dynamic nature of the class interactions, that is, the typical message flows, had to be worked out. This required exploration of the framework at a detailed level by someone who understood something of the way in which CICS works. This again meant that the encapsulated mechanisms were unnecessarily exposed.

- Our experience demonstrated that the use of a framework to develop applications improves productivity. The experience also emphasized the need for the support documentation to fully exploit the productivity potential of such a framework.

8

Object-Oriented Databases

In this chapter we describe the requirements for persistent information in an object-oriented environment and explain how object-oriented databases address those requirements.

8.1 Persistent Objects

The programs written in object-oriented programming languages are similar to programs written in other languages in their handling of data streams. Most languages provide methods to read data from or write data to printers, terminals, and files. Object-oriented programs may also need to store and retrieve objects that must last longer than the execution time of the program that invokes them.

Some languages provide solutions that may be valid for certain types of applications, but are of limited scope. Smalltalk/V, for instance, provides facilities to save a complete image of its current state, including the values for all the variables in the objects of the current application. When the system is restarted, the internal status of the objects is restored to that same state. Smalltalk/V can also write an object into a file as a string from which the object can be reconstructed. These alternatives are not adequate for a multiuser environment. Such an environment requires data uniqueness, security, and integrity, which only database management systems can provide.

One solution is the use of relational database management systems (RDBMs), which can take the object data structure and store it in a relational database. The mapping from objects to tables is not trivial: a class can map to one or more tables, and a table may correspond to more than one class. An association may or may not map to a table, depending on the type and multiplicity of the association and the database designer's preferences in terms of extensibility, number of tables, and performance trade-offs [RUM91]. In addition, there are several approaches for mapping generalizations to tables.

Another problem is that, given the limited support of data types provided by the relational model, it is feasible to store the object data but not the object methods. The types of object data that can be stored are also limited. There are extensions to the relational model that address these limitations, such as the support for **binary large objects** (BLOBs). BLOBs are files that contain binary information representing an image, a procedure, a complex structure, or anything else that does not fit well in a relational database [TAY92]. The database contains references to those files and manages them in an indirect way.

There are limitations to the use of BLOBs because they are physically out of the database environment, and they cannot contain other BLOBs. In addition, data and methods cannot be differentiated. Nevertheless, there are many advantages to using the relational model, such as the availability of set operations and the associative access to data, which avoids the complexity of navigating in a database. These advantages fostered the development of systems such as STARBURST, developed at the IBM Almaden Research Center, and POSTGRES, from the University of California at Berkeley, that are starting to implement such extensions to the relational model.

8.2 Object Database Management Systems

Object database management systems (ODBMSs), designed for the purpose of storing and sharing objects, are another solution for persistent object handling. There is no standard object model yet, and there is no universally acknowledged standard for an ODBMS. There is, however, some commonality in the architecture of the different ODBMSs, because of three necessary components: *object managers, object servers,* and *object stores.* The applications interact with object managers, which work through object servers to gain access to object stores [TAY92].

The ***object manager*** manages a local cache of objects for an *individual* application. The local object cache, usually implemented in virtual memory, acts as a temporary workspace where applications can check out objects from the database. The creation of new objects and the modification of existing objects are performed in the cache first and committed to the database when completed. In addition, the object manager, with the help of the object server, performs the required translations between the formats of the program objects and the formats of the database objects.

Data transfers between database memory and program memory are automatic and transparent to the user. The database detects any reference in a running program to persistent data, and automatically transfers the page containing the referenced data.

All pointers in an application take the form of regular, virtual-memory pointers. A pointer that points to a persistent object initially has as its value a virtual-memory address that is so far unmapped. When the application dereferences the pointer, the operating system signals a violation, which is handled by the database. When an object created by a program is first stored in a database, all the pointers it contains are stored in their original form. When the an object is mapped back into virtual memory, the pointers it contains may have to be altered. Due to the preassignment strategy, every pointer a program uses is either a valid, currently mapped virtual-memory address, or is the virtual memory address that will be occupied by the persistent object the pointer refers to. Figure 8.1 shows a virtual memory implementation of an OODB. An object can reside on one page, alone or together with other objects, or, if large enough, it can span several pages. For fast retrieval, clusters of objects can be defined.

The ***object server*** manages a separate cache of objects that can be shared by many applications. Through this cache, the object server coordinates access to the object store through locking mechanisms. Since there is no initial limitation on what an object can be, some objects, such as CAD drawings, may require longer checkout times than others. Hence, transactions on an ODBMS can have different meaning and duration from those on a business-oriented RDBMS. The locking mechanism should be able to handle short as well as long transactions.

The ***object store*** is the physical storage system, the actual database that resides on disk.

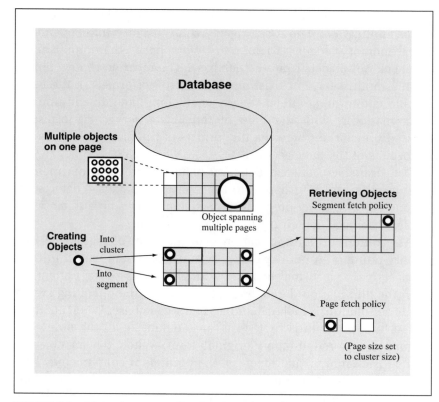

FIGURE 8.1   Virtual-memory implementation of an OODB

Data and Languages: The Impedance Mismatch

As with any other DBMS, ODBMSs need a data definition language (DDL) and a data manipulation language (DML). The alternative here is that the DDL and DML can be defined as extensions of the application programming language, or as built-in languages, inherent to the ODBMS. The problem is that if an ODBMS requires a language different from the application programming language for database access, a significant amount of execution time can be wasted copying data from the database language format to the programming language format and back again [CAT91]. This is called the *impedance mismatch.* However, if the DDL and DML are extensions of a particular language, such as C++, this database is not directly accessible to a program written in another language, for instance, Smalltalk/V. A built-in database language may provide a canonical form for dealing with persistent objects independently of the language in which they were originally defined.

Methods

Methods are handled in different ways in ODBMSs. Some systems store them in the database; others keep them in external files. Storing methods in the database makes it easier to extend existing DBMSs to handle objects. When methods are stored directly in the database and dynamic binding is supported by the programming language, it is not necessary to update objects and methods concurrently. External file handling introduces a requirement for maintenance synchronization. When a class is updated in the database, there may also be a requirement to update the methods in the external file, and vice versa.

ODBMSs in the Marketplace

Objectivity/DB™ from Objectivity, OpenODB™ from Hewlett-Packard, Ontos™ from Ontos Corporation, GemStone™ from Servio Corporation, VERSANT ODBMS™ from Versant Object Technology, and ObjectStore™ from Object Design International are some of the ODBMSs currently available in the marketplace. Some of them are of a general nature, and others support specific types of applications, such as CAD. Some have their own DDLs and DMLs, while others support applications in a specific language environment such as Smalltalk or C++. Most of the implementations support multiuser development and execution through client/server computing.

8.3 The Object-Oriented Database as a Repository

One of the major promises of object orientation is to increase productivity in the application development shop by enabling the reuse of components at different phases of the life cycle, mainly analysis, design, and coding. Models, frameworks, and classes should be stored in a common repository, and analysts, designers, and programmers, directly or by means of CASE tools, should be able to check out these components for reuse in new applications. Because ODBMSs are designed to store objects, it is natural for a repository to be constructed using an object-oriented database.

The main issues to be solved refer to the language neutrality of such a repository, the definition of a common object model, the versioning and browsing capabilities, and the acceptance of a set of standard services, such as those defined by the Portable Common Tools Environment (PCTE) standard developed by the European Computer Manufacturers Association. IBM has made public its intention to provide compliance with PCTE. Because a variety of tool vendors in the areas of analysis, design, and code generation are already developing to the PCTE specifications, this adherence will enable an object-oriented repository to store and manage the data required so that multiple tools can share each other's results [LOO92].

Another Technology: Extended Relational DBMS

The widespread use of relational databases has prompted many organizations to look for a transition path to object technology that does not require a major conversion of their existing data repositories. In many cases, a relational database has been used successfully to "dematerialize" objects, that is, to store their attribute values in the cells of relational tables, and later retrieve the object data to recreate ("materialize") the object. This technique requires a good design. There are many performance implications in the choices that have to be made, but it is a feasible and compatible solution, particularly useful in the case of business applications.

The relational database technology has many advantages. It provides a simple data model based on the use of tables, their columns and rows, integrity constraints, and so forth. It also provides a set-operations query language, with which the user specifies just *what* to retrieve, not *how* to do it: no navigation through the database is necessary.

On the other hand, the relational database has some deficiencies that become more apparent when handling objects. In addition to handling only simple data types, such as integer, real, and string, the relational model does not support complex nested data; there is a limit of one data value per table cell, and cells cannot be navigated via memory pointers. In addition, the relational database management systems are intended to handle short transactions. Managing long transactions is beyond the scope of these systems, as is handling temporal data, history, data versions, and data semantics as defined by object methods.

The ***extended relational DBMS*** provides a relational data model and a query language that has been extended to include extended types, procedures, object identity, and a type hierarchy [CAT91]. These databases use a model that subsumes the relational model, providing compatibility with relational database systems. Figure 8.2 shows the coverage of the requirements of object-oriented programming languages by extended relational databases. Many of the requirements, such as the storing of objects and the handling of extended types and methods can be achieved. Other requirements, such as pointer navigation, are not supported easily by this technology. There

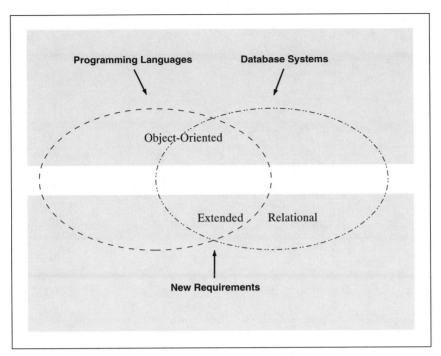

FIGURE 8.2   Database management systems evolution

is no standard today that defines the extended relational model. The SQL3 ANSI standard, when published, is expected to unify the approaches to this technology.

8.4 Summary

- Object-oriented applications require the handling of persistent objects, that is, the storage and retrieval of objects that have to last longer than the program execution time.

- Technologies supporting persistent objects include relational databases, object databases, and extended relational databases.

- Object databases are better adapted to an object-oriented programming language than databases based on the relational model.

- Relational databases have set operations that allow for better query implementations, but are limited in the types they support.

- Extended relational databases seem to subsume the advantages of object and relational databases, but there is not much experience yet with their use in production environments.

9

Industry Standards

In this chapter we describe the ongoing efforts to standardize the treatment of objects to facilitate their compatibility across languages and platforms. International or industrywide standards are not a prerequisite to commercial development of object-oriented applications, but standards of design and coding that apply within an enterprise are. It is sensible to be aware of both. Conforming to industry standards can ensure a long life for the tools and skills; enforcing one's own standards is necessary for successful exploitation of object technology.

Successful and productive work can be performed now without waiting for international standards to be endorsed. However, such work, though initially effective, could turn out to be incompatible with future developments. The rapid development of object technology makes that danger appear greater.

Far-sighted attempts are being made, however, to ensure a head start in standards and therefore in future compatibility. These have found expression in the formation of the Object Management Group, whose proposals are appearing in advance of their being needed. Thus, unlike some other standards efforts, it has not been a matter of merely endorsing a particular product or producer's preeminence in the marketplace. As a result, there have so far been few squabbles among software vendors, who are relied on to implement the standards.

9.1 The Object Management Group

The central purpose of the Object Management Group (OMG) is to create a standard that realizes interoperability among independently developed applications across heterogeneous networks of computers. The Object Management Group's central mission is to establish an architecture and set of specifications, based on commercially available object technology, to enable distributed, integrated applications. Primary goals are the reusability, portability, and interoperability of object-based software components in distributed, heterogeneous environments.

The Object Management Group is a multicompany organization that includes IBM, SUN, Hewlett-Packard, and more than 300 other software vendors, dedicated to producing specifications for commercially available object-oriented environments. The OMG is organized not as a formal standards group, but along the more flexible lines of an industry consortium. It does not plan to build or market products that implement the standards on which it agrees; it will simply define the specifications for its members and others to follow. Each member has agreed to actively support and conform to OMG endorsements in its own commercial offerings. Most notable about the OMG is the speed at which it has moved and the remarkable degree of support for its draft proposals it has so far managed to achieve.

There are two basic models within the OMG's scheme of the object-oriented world [OMG90]. One is the Object Model, which describes the relationships, attributes, and operations of an object and helps provide a conceptual framework for proposed technologies. The other is the Reference Model, which defines the components that are required to make objects function together. The Reference Model can be divided into four elements:

- Object Request Broker, which provides an infrastructure that allows objects to communicate, regardless of the specific platforms and techniques used to implement the objects being addressed.

- Object Services, providing standard functions that objects require to support their existence—for example, integrity, storage, instantiation.

- Common Facilities, providing more standard functions, but at the level of generic application functions, such as database access, printing facilities, security, error reporting, and help.

- Application Objects, which correspond more to the traditional notion of an application, representing related function, such as electronic office or CAD systems.

These potential definitions do not represent interfaces that *must* be used. They simply guarantee interoperability with other objects developed within the same architecture. Thus, one should be able to implement an object or set of objects in Smalltalk/V and be confident that, if the implementation complies with the OMG standards, those objects will be able to use the services of other objects, perhaps implemented in C++ on a physically remote system. Encapsulation will be retained—the application developer of an object-oriented application does not need to know or care about the implementation of these other objects. Most important, this will provide the common basis for reusable class libraries that could be simply purchased and "dropped into" one's own environment with confidence.

Of all these standards, the Object Request Broker (ORB) is the first one to be fully defined and to have at least one vendor implementation. The ORB is explored below in further detail, because it is highly relevant to the direction that object technology is taking and to the speed with which it is being standardized with total vendor independence.

9.2   The Object Request Broker

The ORB is a specification for a system that will manage the communications among objects—managing location, naming and delivery services, activation and deactivation of remote objects, method invocation, parameter encoding, synchronization, exception handling, and security. It sits on top of a network or remote procedure-call mechanism but does not get involved in the applications or (usually) the structure, form, or capabilities of the objects themselves.

Quite simply, the ORB receives a request for a specific operation, finds the appropriate object and methods to process the request, and passes the parameters specified in the request. Then the ORB conveys the results back to the requester or somewhere else. Naturally, the ORB must support many functions in order to execute this simple operation consistently and effectively, but they are hidden from the user of the ORB.

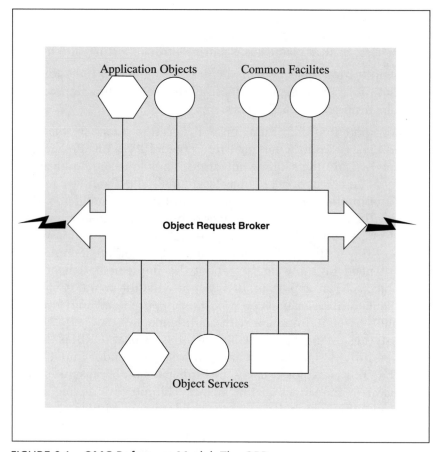

FIGURE 9.1   OMG Reference Model: The ORB

Thus, the ORB provides a framework for cross-system communication between objects. This is the first technical step toward interoperability of object systems. The goal with the ORB is to move from point-to-point local communications to hubs. Everyone can talk to everyone through some common syntax and traffic systems, without needing to understand anything about their partners except for the external interface. Thus encapsulation is maintained.

Figure 9.1 shows the types of objects that are considered in the architecture definition of the OMG object reference model. The objects that pertain to the application domain, the service objects for this application, and the objects that provide common facilities used by all applications.

Most current software systems assume that the application developer is working within an all-encompassing environment, although mechanisms for calling outside exist, for example, in SQL. An ORB allows objects to hide their implementation details for communication outside their own worlds just as they do inside those worlds. In essence, an ORB lets objects encapsulate the outside world and the communications mechanisms, and it encapsulates the objects themselves for the outside world to use. In short, it extends the benefits of object orientation across platforms and communication channels.

This alone, however, does not guarantee interoperability. Two object systems cannot exchange messages successfully unless their object brokers can physically communicate. Also, the ORB addresses the syntax, not the semantics, of the interobject communications. Developers may not need to know the details of implementation if they are addressing an object, but they do need to know the details of the behavior the object will exhibit when a message is sent to it, and the parameters the message needs. The ORB is just a standard for a component; it cannot overcome incompatibilities in the rest of the world. No standard object model has yet been associated with it (although the OMG is addressing the issue).

The OMG's first standard in this area is the Common Object Request Broker Architecture (CORBA) issued in late 1991. In order to support language independence, mappings from the Interface Definition Language (IDL) to a wide variety of programming languages are necessary. This allows programs written in many source languages to interoperate with other applications via CORBA. Agreement on CORBA suggests that systems may be available within a couple of years that will enable real transparent interchange of messages across heterogeneous environments.

The net effect of this is that the different implementations of the technology that are certain to appear from the many firms working in the area should not threaten the goal of achieving greater intersystem compatibility with object-oriented systems than the compatibility achieved currently by non-object-oriented systems across existing environments. That is, objects ought to be able to communicate with one another across machine, software, and vendor boundaries in the same way and with the same intrinsic integrity as they would if they were near neighbors. In the meantime, a development department of an enterprise should implement its own way of communicating in its own environment in the expectation that it can replace its functions with an ORB implementation later, if required.

9.3 Other Areas of Interest

In addition to task forces concerned with the definition of the ORB (CORBA and its successors), the Object Model, and Object Services, other groups are exploring areas of general concern. These include, at present, a group evaluating analysis and design methods, one looking at a common standard for Smalltalk, and another considering standard class libraries for the common object-oriented languages.

These groups do not produce OMG standards; rather they are expected to bring documents to the Technical Committee for a vote. Thus, they indicate potential directions rather than commitment.

9.4 IBM's System Object Model (SOM)

IBM has defined the System Object Model (SOM) as the basis for a multiplatform, distributed object computing environment. It includes OMG's CORBA-compliant, distributed object-management services. It is available for OS/2 today, but is expected to be soon extended to all IBM platforms, and it has been accepted by many other vendors.

It is obvious that if a development group uses two different languages, say Smalltalk and C++, the classes implemented in one language cannot be readily used in another. To provide a solution for such problems, SOM supports the definition, construction, and use of object-oriented programs independently of the programming languages in which they have been coded. It does not replace programming languages: it provides a language-neutral common library that applications written in different languages can use.

SOM makes object technology binary-compatible [RYM93]; that is, class libraries distributed as DLL objects in applications can be used or replaced, without having to recompile the whole environment. Binary compatibility is not new for procedures, but it is for object-oriented class libraries, and it is essential for the practical use of object-oriented application frameworks.

DSOM (Distributed SOM) is a component of SOM that supports transparent remote access to objects in a distributed environment. It is CORBA-compliant and implements the CORBA static and dynamic interfaces. Using DSOM, SOM applications can access an object via a direct reference called a *handle.* If the handle is local, the reference maps to the actual object. If the object is remote, the reference maps to a proxy object that takes the request and delivers it to the remote object, which in turn is managed by an object adapter.

The SOM environment also includes the Persistent Framework, which defines an object storage and retrieval facility. SOM may later include Application Frameworks, such as graphics, multimedia, word and speech processing frameworks developed by IBM and other companies.

9.5 Summary

- The object-oriented paradigm provides an excellent foundation for a transparent client/server computing environment, but to achieve that end, standards are important and must be generally accepted.

- Many efforts at different levels—international, industry-wide, and industry-specific—have been made to standardize the communications among objects produced by programs written in different languages on different platforms.

- The OMG is today the major player in object-oriented standardization.

- The OMG ORB specification sets the standard for interoperability among different platforms.

- IBM's SOM is a robust implementation of the OMG CORBA standard.

10

The Management of Object-Oriented Projects

In this chapter we analyze the particular aspects of the management of object-oriented projects, such as the development approach (including the process model and the chosen methodology), the use of prototyping, and the need to achieve the productivity enhancements promised by reuse. Those aspects affect the staffing of the MIS group, especially the project team organization, the required training, the need for a development environment, including languages and CASE and configuration-management tools. For development environments based on reuse, there is not much experience in the estimation of costs and development schedules.

10.1 Management Concerns

MIS managers who understand the productivity gains and quality achievement promised by the object-oriented paradigm are nevertheless concerned with many areas in which no easy decision path exists. They know that the waterfall process model does not work, but spiral or incremental development, with its interaction requirements, is often foreign to the corporate culture. There are also numerous methodologies on the market, and none of them is the clear winner. Most of the available object-oriented CASE tools are only good for drawing and documenting. Their code-generating capabilities are rather limited, and small-team programmers do not use them at all. In addition, basing the development activity on prototyping is perceived as threatening because of a potential loss of control.

Human factors are another area of concern. Development team members need time to become familiar with procedural languages, to learn the "the new way of thinking" that object orientation requires. There is never enough time for object-oriented training, and there are not many experiences to lean on. The most difficult problem is probably to deal with the "not invented here" syndrome, and to motivate reuse and the creation of reusable components.

What Is Reusable?

Object technology facilitates the reuse of the inputs and outputs of most of the development phases. In analysis, the specifications and the models may be reused, as well as the data dictionary. The models may be reusable as a whole or, in addition, at the individual class level. In design, reuse may occur again at the model or class level, or at the level of identified design patterns [HEL93] and subsystem definitions. In the coding phase, we may reuse classes implemented in specific programming languages, class libraries, and frameworks. Test cases and scenarios can also be reused, as well as documentation templates.

The possibility of reusing components requires establishing and maintaining a repository of reusable "products." The use of a repository implies a definition of what goes into the repository, how the components are checked-in, how ownership is determined, how components are later accessed, and what rules apply to component modification. In addition, communication and promotional mechanisms must be established. Developers should be aware of the availability of reusable components and their meaning and purpose, and they should be rewarded for reuse.

The efficient management of object-oriented projects therefore requires managers to define and implement a reuse process model [GOL92] that describes such activities as identifying the need for an application, deciding if it should be built in-house or purchased, defining mechanisms to certify component quality, store a component in the repository, access it, and communicate about its availability.

There should be also a mechanism to assess whether a component is useful in a given situation, and to determine how to use and maintain components.

Staffing for Reuse

Reuse does not happen naturally. Special efforts are required in any phase that produces components intended for reuse, in order to ensure and facilitate their reusability. These efforts are related not only to the actual delivery of the components, but also to their documentation and maintenance, and to the way of informing the development team of their existence.

The reuse process requires organizational changes in the MIS department to support it. In addition to the traditional functions of project leader, architect or chief designer, analyst, designer, programmer and system support, new roles are required. Some of them can be filled by existing members who acquire the new skills, but others require the creation of new positions within the organization. For instance, an existing architect can become an object-oriented architect with additional training. Prototyping skills may already exist in an organization that has left behind the waterfall model, and a distinction between analysis and design prototypes may already have been recognized by the MIS organization, and so on.

Reuse, however, requires a separate role assignment in order to be successful. There is the need to acquire, evaluate, and classify the newly created reusable components, ensuring that they meet the quality, style, documentation, and applicability criteria set by the organization. Information about the new available components must be communicated to the development team. In addition, help should be available for developers who need to locate or access reusable components on request. The function of reuse administrator and/or reuse manager is therefore required.

MIS management should support reuse by providing incentives for developers to participate. A developer who is paid by the number of lines of code written has no reason to reuse anything. From a maintenance point of view, the less new code is written, the better. The ideal situation would be to have a rich set of high-quality components that could be put together in many ways in order to build new applications, since the less code programmers write, the less errors they will introduce. Thus, it is productive to have an incentive policy, that rewards application developers for meeting deadlines and for the percentage of components reused.

The existence of a formal reuse process is an indication of the maturity of the organization, and this is naturally so. A team that is just starting to develop applications with object technology has nothing to reuse. Recognizing the reusability of components comes with the practice, but should not be left to chance. The reuse team that should be put in place once serious object-oriented development is underway is a key element in the success expected from the paradigm shift.

10.2 The Transition to Object Technology

The transition to object technology requires addressing several key questions at the corporate level. These questions concern the opportunity of such a transition, as well as costs, resource allocation, and the preservation of the investment in existing systems. Since object technology involves a paradigm shift, the transfer of the technology to the organization is a key issue for success.

Transfer of Technology

The process of transferring a new technology to an organization is not linear: the needs of the target organization vary during the process, depending on the phase of the transfer the organization is involved in. Four transfer phases can be identified from the point of view of the target organization [TKA93]:

1. Awareness: the target organization should know about the existence of the new technology and understand the advantages and risks involved in embracing it.

2. Exploration: the target organization sets-up prototype projects using the new technology.

3. Transition: the target organization has decided to embrace the new technology, and the existing technology base is being converted to the new one.

4. Habit: the new technology has become "business as usual" in the target organization. A mature stage of this phase would be characterized by the presence of process control, quality standards, and productivity measurements.

The awareness phase is the key to achieving an effective transfer of technology. This phase is particularly crucial for object technology, since many economic and cultural decisions have to be made. The recipients of the transfer in this phase are both managers and programmers.

Managers and programmers have to be aware of the advantages of object technology and the requirements for capitalizing on these advantages. The bottom line is that productivity and quality in object-oriented software development are achieved through reuse, but then the meaning and nature of reuse must be understood, as well as the organizational changes it entails. Technical decision issues such as the choice of language and methodology have to be explained, but should not become the focus at this point. It is more important to deal with the "not invented here" syndrome, and with legitimate concerns such as incentives, performance evaluations, and training opportunities.

The main objective of the transfer of technology in the awareness phase is that the technology should not be perceived as threatening by anyone but as a growth opportunity for everyone. Short courses (from one to five days) that include technology fundamentals, advantages, technical and organizational considerations, success stories (both internal and external), and marketplace trends and directions, are effective transfer means in this phase. Those courses should be delivered in-house, and there should be several opportunities to attend them on different dates; a teach-the-teachers session by company experts or external consultants may be a convenient way to start the process. A list of recommended conferences and trade shows may be a useful tool for stirring the interest of key people in the target organization.

The exploration phase is characterized by the existence of "points of light" or "negative entropy pockets," that is, small nuclei of developers that test the new technology, many times with manager consent during normal working hours, but often after hours. Enthusiasts of the new technology appear, probably with some background from the university, from readings, or from previous jobs. The transfer of technology in this phase requires the definition of a specific development environment, the availability of such an environment, and the training of selected people in its use for concrete pilot projects. User's groups, where the practitioners of the new technology and interested people meet, say, once per month, to discuss topics, present their projects and even invite external speakers, have proven to be successful in the transfer of technology in this stage.

In the transition phase, the key issue is productivity. The technology required now, in addition to the continuous training efforts, relates to processes, control, and metrics, which usually have to be imported. A source of exchange of sophisticated questions and solutions has to be established, such as e-mail conferences and forums.

In the habit phase, the quest is for refining the technology, improving existing processes, and exploring the next steps. This level justifies the existence of an in-house staff of high-level specialists who determine what aspects of the technology should be transferred, and where.

Although awareness-exploration-transition-habit is a natural sequence, it is by no means a necessary one. The following are three counter-examples describing cases where this sequence will not hold (and many more can be found):

1. A company take-over or merger, where the new owner has already developed object-oriented systems

2. A multinational company that imposes the new technology on its worldwide branches.

3. A start-up company that decides to start developing systems with object technology.

The described sequence is, however, a typical process for any organizational paradigm shift.

Starting an Object-Oriented Project

When an organization has decided to adopt object technology, a decision must be made regarding the selection of some aspect of the business to model using object technology [TAY92]. The choice of the right area and the scale of the model are major factors that will influence the success of the early experiences. As with any new technology, the most prudent attitude is to assess and demonstrate the benefits of object technology with a minimum of risk and disruption. The introduction of a new technology always creates many expectations. Therefore, it is desirable to demonstrate its benefits in a highly visible manner in order to encourage its acceptance in the enterprise. This implies that the first project should be neither trivial nor attack an obscure company process. It should focus on the core business of the organization, so that its relevance to corporate productivity and competitiveness can be tested and made evident.

A safe criterion is to avoid systems integration as much as possible during the proof-of-concept stage in order to reduce the effort involved and protect the company's operations from learning experiences. It is hard to envision a core business application that is totally independent of other business processes, but the integration can be left to a later stage, where it becomes another aspect of the testing of the technology.

The main power and appeal of object technology lie in both the use of common, real-world elements in the requirements, analysis, and design phases, and in the reuse and extension of current development efforts. Therefore, an assessment of object technology should include the building of a model in a preferably familiar application domain, the building of a small library of reusable classes as part of this process, and the implementation of other related applications based on the existing class model and library. Additional assessment tests may include a parallel development using the organization's current technology and a maintenance test involving code modification to meet new requirements. The learning curve should be evaluated independently and compared with the learning curve of the current technology: it can become an important decision factor.

Object-Oriented Integration

One of the key elements in the assessment process is to protect the existing investment in information systems while exploiting the new technology, which may have demonstrated a clear productivity gain. However, the nature of the existing systems should be carefully analyzed. *Existing system components may be as heterogeneous among themselves as they are with respect to the new technology*. Therefore, a good way to improve the quality of an organization's information systems is to start with an objective technology audit.

Studies by the Software Engineering Institute affiliated with Carnegie-Mellon University have shown that most corporate information systems in the United States have been developed primarily on an ad hoc basis. There is little formalization in most applications. Standards and methodologies exist but are practiced "informally" [YOU92], according to the developer's interpretation. There is usually a mixture of databases from several generations of technology, and many applications that access these databases were developed in different languages by developers who left the company long ago. Some applications are poorly documented, and some are not documented at all. The use of development tools is not universal, and information system resources are overburdened with the hand-crafted maintenance of legacy code. Legacy code systems are usually loosely coupled, sometimes at the database level, more often at the application level. Therefore, the meaning of the integration concept must be clearly defined.

A complete rebuilding of existing applications is not considered within the realm of any technology. In that context, object technology provides several approaches for easing the transition, and for integrating the new object-oriented software with existing systems.

- Wrapper technology, which provides an object-oriented interface to legacy code. The wrapped piece of legacy code behaves as an object. This technology is useful, but the legacy code may not be able to take advantage of existing resources. For instance, it may access files by an obsolete method.

- Reverse-engineering technology, which aims to discover the design and the specifications from the legacy code. In terms of object-oriented modeling, it implies taking the legacy code and building a model, and then developing the new system from the basis of that model. Since the original system was not developed with object technology, it is not possible to determine the assumptions and alternatives that went into the analysis and design of that software.

- Incremental updating, which can be considered an object-oriented version of software reengineering. This approach consists of analyzing legacy code, especially data-subprogram relationships, and working toward the identification of clusters or partitions by means of statistical techniques [LUK92]. Each cluster becomes a candidate for being modeled as a class. Because the cluster will probably be too big for building a useful model in the first cut, the same technique can be applied to each of the new classes, trying to identify the means of encapsulation. This task will probably benefit from the use of code-slicing tools.

Legacy code is not the only information systems element that requires integration. Existing models at the enterprise, business-area, and application levels can provide input to the object-oriented modeling process, as described in Section 3.3, "Structured Analysis Methodologies." The reverse process is also possible and leads to a different level of integration. Starting from an object analysis of the business system, the normalized states of certain objects can become entities without loss of meaning, because objects encapsulate both states and behavior.

10.3 Summary

- The characteristics of object technology present a challenge to the management of the development environment. In particular, reuse requires a different system of staffing, measuring and incentives than a conventional software project.

- Object technology can be learned and assessed independently, but integration with the existing information structure is a fundamental requirement.

- Several techniques that can ease the transition must be carefully evaluated for each case. The transition period of coexistence of the different technologies should be evaluated.

- Extensions to present development tools, information and data models, and even standards will probably facilitate the transition to object technology by providing a convergent approach.

11

A Roadmap for Development

Object technology provides for productive application development. The object-oriented analysis phase produces a real-world model in which many classes have the same semantics as the entities defined in E-R modeling. Pure object-oriented analysis techniques, such as OMT or those described by Coad and Yourdon, have their roots in modern information-modeling technologies, where the main emphasis is on data structure analysis as opposed to the function analysis advocated by early structured methodologies.

This book does not intend to add a new object-oriented analysis and design methodology to the existing methodologies. In order to show the development of an application with object orientation, however, we describe here a roadmap to application development that is compatible in principle with information-modeling concepts, such as those described by AD/Cycle.

This roadmap includes a list of activities that use modeling as a starting point (see Figure 11.1). According to the methodology used, the modeling step can produce an object model or an E-R model. This step can be omitted if E-R modeling has already been done. If not, and if a pure object-oriented analysis and design methodology is chosen,

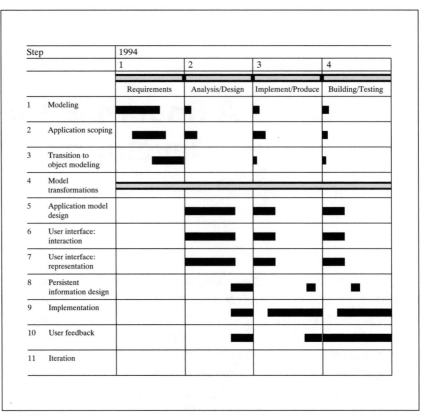

FIGURE 11.1   Schedule for the object-oriented application development roadmap

then Step 3, Transition to Object Modeling, is not required.

The steps of an object-oriented development process are not intended to be executed in a strict sequential order. Although some steps depend on the deliverables of others, the phases overlap (as described, for instance, by the iterative life cycle model), and each step may influence any other. This leads to refinement and better approximation of the application requirements, and a better understanding and mapping of user needs.

11.1 Step 0: Requirements

Before starting the development of an application it is necessary to establish the requirements. Creating a short statement of system purpose, from the perspective of both the user and the expert, helps focus the design team on solving the problem. This statement can be based on the results of meetings and interviews with users, experts, and managers, or it can be provided by the requester of the system. The statement should reflect what is needed, not how it should be done.

Once a purpose statement has been written, a requirements statement can be developed. This should include, in addition to the purpose, guidelines on the scope of the application and its context, assumptions, performance, and security needs.

11.2 Step 1: Modeling

The objective of Step 1 is to build a model that shows the static data structure of the real-world system and organizes it into workable pieces [RUM91]. To construct a model, the relevant entities or classes must be identified from the application domain. These include physical entities, such as computers, persons, and cars, and conceptual entities, such as manufacturing schedules and bank accounts. The entities defined should belong to the application domain or the real world; they should not be computer implementation constructs, such as arrays.

The syntactical analysis of the requirements statement is the basis for identifying the model entities. Entities and classes often correspond to nouns, although they may also correspond to attributes. Nouns may be generic, such as *car,* or may correspond to an individual object or example, such as "My Ford Taurus," in which case a generic word (*car, vehicle*) should be chosen to represent the entity. The original set so determined should be pruned to discard unnecessary and incorrect entities.

Relationships or associations describe dependencies between two or more entities. They occur in the requirements statement as verb phrases or link phrases between nouns. For example, *A car has four wheels* (Has) or *A purchase order is approved by the clerk* (Approved-by). Relationships are defined only between existing entities; therefore, if a noun was discarded as a source of an entity, the prospective relationship should also be discarded. The possible multiplicity of the relationship, such as one-to-one and one-to-many (a company has one chief executive officer; a person has one car but may have many), should also be considered.

The attributes of the entities or classes can be found by looking in the statement for nouns followed by possessive phrases, for example, *the color of the house* (color) or *the number of pages of the book* (number of pages). An attribute should depend on the existence of an entity. If it exists in its own right, it is better modeled as a separate entity.

The deliverable of this step is either an object model or an E-R model, depending on the methodology chosen. If a methodology is to be chosen, object-oriented modeling is recommended. In that case, the modeling task requires looking at not only the plausible entities but their behaviors and responsibilities to each other. Analysis, together with a dynamic approach such as use case modeling [JAC92] and object behavior analysis [GIB90] provide a very efficient combination for finding the correct objects. If E-R modeling is an already developed in-house skill, it may be used in this step, while performing a conversion to object modeling as described in Step 3. To illustrate this conversion, an E-R approach was chosen for modeling the Game application (see Appendix B, "The Game: An Example").

11.3   Step 2: Application Scoping

The scope of the model built in Step 1 is usually wider than the user originally required. It is therefore necessary to determine the scope of the application. This should generally be done as a first-level approximation of the development of the prototype defined in each iteration (as described by the spiral life cycle model). The general scoping is to be considered only as a first-level approximation because the final scope of the application will be determined by whatever new requirements are prompted by the user's experience with the prototypes.

Interfaces with the Non-Object-Oriented Environment   It may be necessary in this step to define the integration between the application to be developed and existing legacy code. This integration can be implemented in several ways, including the use of object-oriented programming language code in modules of non-object-oriented systems or the wrapping of legacy code that is included as an object in an object-oriented application.

Interfaces with Databases   There is a relation between an E-R model and a *relational* model. Therefore, if persistent object data from the application is to be stored in a relational database, the database design can be started from the model. There is really no standard E-R model, and since a class model can be considered as an enhanced form of an E-R model with the addition of several new concepts, a mapping between objects and relational tables can be defined. It is important to consider, however, that there is generally no direct 1:1 relation between classes and tables. Each class maps to one or more tables, and a table may correspond to more than one class if the classes are linked with one-to-one or one-to-many associations [RUM91]. In addition, inheritance relations, which do not exist in the E-R model, have to be

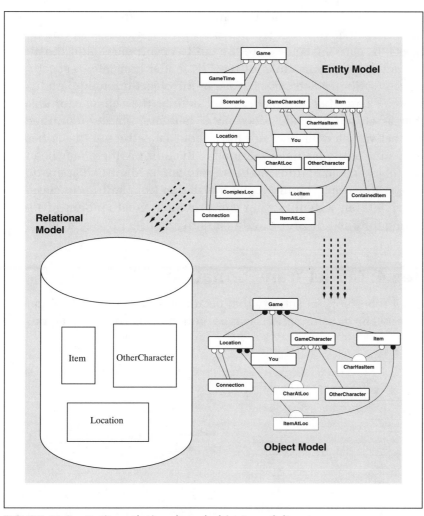

FIGURE 11.2   Entity, relational, and object models

implemented. Figure 11.2 shows the mappings that can be made between the database, the E-R model, and the persistent object model, that is, the part of the object model whose data must be kept from one run of the application to the next. Persistent information design is discussed in Step 8.

11.4 Step 3: Transition to Object Modeling

An entity map can provide the basis for a first cut of classes to build the class diagram of an object-oriented model. Many entities may map to classes; in that case, the mapping rule is that for each entity in the entity map that has defined attributes, a class can be defined. The objects, or class instances, are the entity occurrences, and the attributes and dependency links of the E-R model translate, respectively, into the attributes and associations of the object-oriented paradigm.

Remember that an object model defines the behavior of objects, whereas an entity model does not. Therefore, objects identified by their active behavior may not have their data structure described by an existing entity from the E-R model. In addition, there may be many more objects than entities, since objects can be identified at many levels of abstraction. Therefore, the translation from entities to classes is not trivial, but an entity map can provide a great amount of useful starting information and should certainly be used, if available.

11.5   Step 4: Model Transformations

Step 4 represents an activity that occurs throughout the development process. The transformations can be motivated by conceptual grouping

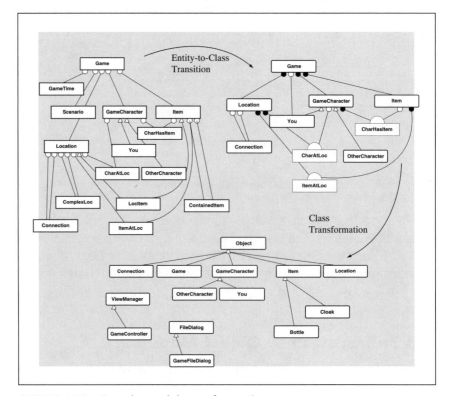

FIGURE 11.3   Sample model transformations

considerations or by design and implementation needs (see Figure 11.3).

Class transformations due to conceptual grouping may involve:

- Grouping simpler classes into more complex classes.
- Classifying classes into hierarchies.

There are many design reasons for adding classes and relations or defining hierarchies. For instance, one may want to construct **container** classes, that is, classes used as data structures that can contain a number of elements.

A main difference between classes and entities is that the data structures in the classes are *encapsulated* by the (access) methods or operations. These methods are defined in Step 5.

11.6   Step 5: Application Model Design

The objects defined in the object model now require a detailed plan to determine the details for computer implementation. This step corresponds to the design of the model part of the model-view-controller framework.

Model design includes the design of algorithms to implement operations, optimization of access paths to data, adjustments of the inheritance hierarchy, implementation of associations, and definition of the representation of attributes. In addition, new classes may be created during this step: those classes are not modeling the real world, but they are convenient to have for computational reasons and should be defined here.

11.7   Step 6: User Interface: Interaction

Step 6 focuses on the design of the controller part of the model-view-controller framework.

Control Styles

There are several *control styles* that relate to the way objects interact. The possibilities in the implementation are determined by the facilities of the implementation language and the operating system. There are also external and internal levels of control that deal with interobject communication and the underlying process flow. At this stage only the external process flow is relevant.

The control style chosen for object-oriented application design is usually event-driven, which requires the existence of a controller class. During the design, the sequence of events that defines the business processes is the guideline that determines the user tasks, which are used in the design of a controller class structure. The controller is a representation of the user tasks. It takes care of the synchronization requirements. The controller-class map reflects the global application structure.

The rationale for specifying separate classes to represent user task structures is to reduce the coupling between the Model and View classes, making that coupling less process-dependent, and therefore making the classes more suitable for reuse.

Many techniques can be used to design the controller class. The next section describes one of them, the use of message flows.

Message Flows

Objects encapsulate behavior, which is implemented by methods or operations. Those methods are invoked by means of messages. To define the methods for a given object (class) it is useful to prepare scenarios of typical interaction sequences and identify the events that occur between objects [RUM91]. For each scenario, an event trace can be prepared. This event trace corresponds to the message flow between objects, since each event can be represented as a message. In the case of external events, such as keyboard typing or mouse clicking, it is useful to define an event-handler object that translates external events to message flows to other objects, such as a window.

The events that reach an object can change its internal states. The methods of an object can be derived from the message flow diagram and the state changes in that object.

11.8 Step 7: User Interface: Representation

Step 7 focuses on the view part of the model-view-controller framework. What a user sees on the screen is a window showing the information stored in the model. The way this information is displayed in that window, that is, the *view,* has therefore an essential dependency on the model.

User participation is very important at every stage of the development process, particularly for the design of the user interface. The term *user,* in this case, refers not only to the primary or operational user but also to all other users who require the results of the operation for their processes. For instance, in the design of an automated ticket seller for railways, the user guidance information that appears in a screen does not include usage statistics because they are irrelevant for the customer, who is the primary user. Those statistics, however, are important to the planning department, which expects the system to collect them. The bottom line is that for application modeling, the user's screen is an important element, but not the only one. When the system is complex, or when it has to serve the needs of several users, an application must keep track of more than what needs to be shown on the user's screen.

11.9 Step 8: Persistent Information Design

Persistent data is data that is stored from one execution of the program to the next and used in subsequent executions. It has a slightly different connotation from *output data*, that is, data produced by the program that will not be involved in the next execution. The persistent data requirements may refer to some data contained in the object data structure, or to the storing of the structure as a whole. The persistent information model is the object-oriented representation of persistent data. The model is designed by looking at the classes and relationships that must be kept and mapping them to the corresponding persistent store structures.

When mapping object classes to tables, a class can map to one or more tables, and tables can correspond to more than one class. Associations may or may not map to tables. It depends on the type and multiplicity of the association and on database design considerations.

Generalizations (inheritance) require a careful approach. Multiple inheritance should in principle be avoided. Mapping single inheritance generalizations to tables can be done in several ways [RUM91]:

- The superclass and each subclass can map to a table.
- A superclass table is not defined; superclass attributes are replicated for each subclass.
- Subclass tables are not defined; subclass attributes are brought up to the superclass level.

There are advantages and trade-offs to each implementation.

Relational databases are not the only way of storing persistent objects. Object-oriented databases (OODBs) are a new technology that provides a specialized solution to the object-storing requirement. OODBs allow the storing of complete objects (data structures and methods). In addition, some languages and environments provide their own facilities, mostly as application-delivery mechanisms. For instance, the ObjectFiler facility distributed with Smalltalk/V PM is intended for storing and exchanging data objects (but not methods). The choice of the persistent data repository and the requirements for implementation should be carefully considered and defined, if needed, during this step.

11.10 Step 9: Implementation

Although object-oriented modeling can be valuable even if the implementation language is not object-oriented, many benefits arise from using those languages in the context of a spiral or iterative approach. Those benefits arise because the object-oriented programming languages allow the definition of objects and classes that are maintained as recognizable entities during the whole life cycle. That is, the same objects are used in the analysis, design, and coding phases.

There are many object-oriented languages on the market. Currently the two languages that are usually considered at this stage are Smalltalk and C++. Opinion (not always based on facts) suggests that Smalltalk tends to be more useful for GUI design and application prototyping, whereas C++ is more suitable to production implementations. The modern versions of Smalltalk and the available configuration-management tools, however, show that the language is rapidly evolving into an environment suitable for production applications.

C++, with its roots in C, can be expected to be fast-running and robust, but well-balanced, ready-to-use class libraries are not publicly available. There is also a difference between C++ native-compiler implementations and the implementations that use a C compiler with a C++ preprocessor: the code produced by the latter is much more difficult to debug.

The choice of a language in each case depends on considerations regarding application, platform, skills, and software characteristics. There seems to be a growing consensus that because it runs close to the machine and is very fast, C++ is probably a better choice for system programming, real-time transactions, and applications in the scientific and engineering arena. Smalltalk's high-level syntax and transparent memory management make it better suited to mainstream business applications such as manufacturing management and customer service systems [TAY92].

Frameworks, class libraries, workbench environments, screen painters, CASE tools with code generators, browsers, and configuration-management tools can make application development much more productive. They should therefore be considered as key elements in the successful implementation of object technology.

11.11 Step 10: User Feedback

User feedback is the true test of the fidelity of the application to the requirements. The earlier user feedback is solicited, the better.

In most cases, the user feedback, by clarifying the requirements, will prompt some modification in the system, which may be confined to an algorithm or GUI design, or may require changes in the whole model. Iteration is therefore a natural component of the object-oriented application development life cycle.

11.12 Step 11: Iteration

The recommended strategy is to take small steps of development at a time and then go back to the appropriate step of the roadmap (this will sometimes be Step 5, or it may be Step 3 or even Step 1), and iteratively apply what has been learned. At the lower levels of design, the opportunities for reuse may be more apparent. This may have an additional influence on the class generalizations that are done at higher levels of design and on the event analysis. Iteration may span one or more phases of the development process. It may, for instance, be just circumscribed to coding, or require a return to the design phase, which in turn may require changes in the analysis model. The possibility of iteration leads to code that reflects the user requirements better and requires less maintenance.

11.13 Summary

- This chapter describes a roadmap used for the development of object-oriented applications.

- In order to facilitate the transition from information-modeling concepts, this roadmap indicates the possibility of starting from E-R modeling. However, if an E-R model is used, it should be only at the beginning: there is no advantage in simultaneously maintaining object and data models.

- The steps of the roadmap may overlap, and the whole roadmap may be iterated.

Design Notation for Documentation

In this appendix we describe the notation used for documenting the Game example. The notation does not correspond to any particular standard, but it is the one implemented in an internal-use documentation tool that was available for this project. It is a concise notation that presents information in three different ways: the object view, the entity view, and the methods view.

A.1 The Object View

The object view is the most common view of object-oriented information. Figure A.1 depicts the shapes used to document the different classes and the various forms of relationships between classes. A distinction is made between classes, external classes, and relations.

Classes that are part of the model are depicted as bold rectangles with rounded corners. Other classes are present because they indicate how the model relates to a base class tree, or they indicate reused classes. They are called *external* classes, and they are shown as thin rectangles with rounded corners.

The thin rectangles with a half circle on top indicate a relationship. They can be used to describe complex relations between classes. Simple associations are given as lines between two classes with small circles at the parent side. Small solid circles at the parent side describe a one-to-many relationship.

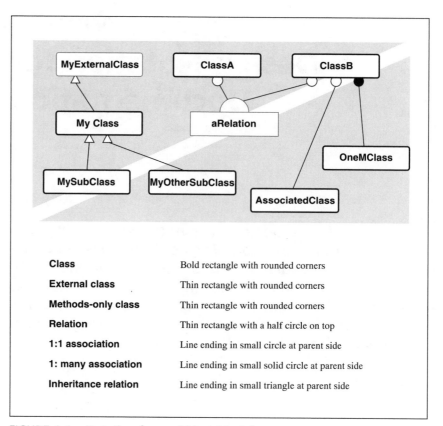

Class	Bold rectangle with rounded corners
External class	Thin rectangle with rounded corners
Methods-only class	Thin rectangle with rounded corners
Relation	Thin rectangle with a half circle on top
1:1 association	Line ending in small circle at parent side
1: many association	Line ending in small solid circle at parent side
Inheritance relation	Line ending in small triangle at parent side

FIGURE A.1   Notation for an Object Model

A.2 The Methods View

The methods view shows both the class names and the method names. Because the methods of a class represent its *responsibilities* the methods view can be used by practitioners of *responsibility-driven design*, as described in [WIR90].

A.3 The Entity View

In the entity view, the notation is a variation of the standard E-R modeling notation, where the only relations allowed are dependency relations. This results in a model that is equivalent to a normalized relational model:

- In Figure A.2, ClassA, ClassB, aRelation, and DependentClass are examples of entities.
- An entity may have attributes that describe its static aspects.

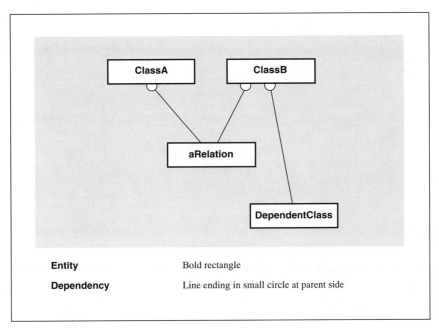

FIGURE A.2   Notation for an entity model

Entities are connected to each other by dependency relations. A dependency indicates that an instance of the parent entity must exist before the dependent entity instance can be created.

In this notation, one-to-one relations and one-to-many relations cannot be differentiated. Complex relationships are modeled as entities. Inheritance relations cannot be described in the entity view. Therefore, the object view is normally used for object-oriented modeling, because it can express a richer set of relationships.

The Game: An Example

This appendix describes the process of developing the prototype of an application with elements of object technology. This project was conceived with the following purposes:

- *To provide a prototype of an interactive tutorial based on object-oriented development concepts.*

- *To illustrate the use of the object-oriented development roadmap*

- *To make clear the concepts of generalized design of applications with reuse in mind.*

The desire was to develop an example that provided an easy way of illustrating the major object-oriented concepts. A game or puzzle presents concepts from the real world that are familiar to everyone, for example, finding one's way in a maze. An object-oriented implementation of a game should therefore show how well object orientation maps that real world (or parts of it).

B.1 The Value of the Example

The illustration of a large application development with small examples can be useful to get an understanding of the technology, but there is always the question of the feasibility of upscaling the example. The object-oriented approach to modeling and the implementation of encapsulation and polymorphism make it possible to look at, prototype, and implement an application at an overview level. Then one can expand the application with the required detailed functionality, such as database handling, error recovery, and distribution, without major changes in the code already built. The expansion is usually incremental, based on the prototype model; more objects are added, or the required access methods are fully implemented.

For example, a prototype can contain some main objects that are sufficient for the proof-of-concept and understanding by the user. The final model will include many more objects from the real world and some of computational origin without really changing the prototyped behavior of the model. In the prototype, the data might be stored in small flat files on the workstation, while the real production application has to support a large corporate host database. In that case, the parts of the application that need reworking are the methods in those classes that actually read data from the files and should now read data from the database. With proper design, the rework to be done is minimal. From the perspective of the business logic, the instantiation of objects from external data would be transparent.

Furthermore, object-orientation derives its importance from the opportunities for reuse. Frameworks, generic applications, and class libraries are the object-oriented way of providing reusable code. For both Smalltalk and C++, an increasing number of these constructs are becoming available in areas such as base language classes, database interface, communication, and user interface building. Business classes can be custom-developed or may be available from framework repositories developed previously at the shop or from vendors. These classes are used initially for fast prototyping. Since they have been tested before, the initial development of the application can focus on the business aspects, rather than on debugging.

The example that follows assumes that there is no initial framework available for the prototyping. The modeling process is started from the beginning; that is, object classes are derived from the problem statement of the application and from interviews with the expert.

B.2 Step 0 of the Roadmap: Requirements

This step comprises the proposal of a formal initial requirements definition.

Information Gathering: Interview with the Expert

The definitions of the initial application domain (game subject matter) were given verbally during an interview with a rather histrionic domain expert called "the Wizard." A transcript of the interview follows:

"So," the Wizard started, by way of preamble, "not everybody is an illusion. Nothing is real."

He pondered his own last remark for a bit. "And there are objects, of course," he added, "objects are real too." "Time is not real, but it is consistent, and that makes it real. Remember that."

This time the pause was quite short. "Mazes are interesting as well," he said, with his eyes sparkling, "they can change you know. Rooms can move and doors can appear and disappear."

He smiled. "Oh, don't worry," he went on, "they can't change when you are inside the maze. The Mazemaster can change the maze when you are not there, but not once you have entered. After all, you are the central character in all this."

After another short period of thought, he went on, "Even the other characters—the ones that live in the maze—cannot do anything unless you do."

His voice became even quieter, "Another great truth is that objects can affect the maze in various ways. Imagine, some objects are not permitted to go through certain doors! And," he went on, "sometimes you are not allowed to go through a door if you do not have a particular object!"

"Of course," the Wizard added, "each object has its own behavior as well—that makes it unique as an object—and that never changes."

"Now," and again, his voice became lower, "the effects that objects have on the maze is another thing that is decided by the Mazemaster. Also (now his voice was no more than the barest whisper), the Mazemaster even decides what tests you must pass in order to complete the maze; and that is the third great truth."

"I can tell you this much," he whispered conspiratorially, "In order to succeed, you must meet each challenge in a certain order, and armed with the appropriate talismans and devices."

The Wizard sat back in his chair. "A piece of advice," he resumed with his voice at a more natural level. "Never take an object totally at face value. Some objects have been known to hide other objects, for example."

A secret smile twitched at the corners of the Wizard's mouth. "The same can be said for locations in the maze, of course," he added, almost as an afterthought.

"And while we are talking about advice," he continued, leaning forward again, "some of the other characters might give you advice from time to time. It is up to you whether you think it good advice," he said, cryptically.

He finally smiled and said, "Or whether you believe that I am more than an illusion too," and then he sat back and promptly went to sleep.

Analysis of the Problem Statement for the Game

The game involves traversing a maze that is made of a number of linked locations (rooms). The system presents the maze to the player one location at a time. The configuration of the maze can be changed from session to session (by the Mazemaster) but remains constant during a given session.

The maze is inhabited by several characters; one of them of a type called You and represents the player. In addition there are items that can be manipulated by the characters: those items may contain or hide other items. The characters move through the maze in an uncontrolled fashion, except the instance of You which we call aYou, and is controlled by the player.

While traversing the maze, aYou needs to carry certain items in order to enter some locations. On the other hand, some objects may not pass through certain doors.

An item or character may be seen only when it is in the same location as aYou. aYou may interrogate the characters or ask for some explanation of the purpose of an item.

The purpose of the game is to complete the steps defined at the beginning (by the Mazemaster) in a certain order, which can be changed from game to game. The player indicates the direction in which he or she wants to move, and the system indicates if that move is valid or not at that time.

This definition documents all of the salient points:

- An adventure game, which implies "flexible" rules.

- One central character, who represents the player (aYou).

- The character has to negotiate through various obstacles in order to reach a variable target.

- The environment is a maze: a bounded space consisting of specific locations that are interconnected.

- The character has to achieve goals (e.g., collect some items) in order to progress through the maze.

- There may be other characters in the game.

B.3 Step 1: Modeling

Step 1 of the roadmap for application development involves finding the entities that belong to the chosen E-R model. This model will be independent of the implementation environment. Although direct object modeling was possible and even advantageous, the example starts by finding the entities of the data model, in order to exemplify the full roadmap. To ease the transition, we used an extended E-R model, which included inheritance relationships (indicated by the white triangles), and also lists the actions associated with each game element (entity).

The main model entities are derived from the following elements, defined in the problem statement:

- There is one central character, who is identified with the user.
- The maze is a static map of interconnected locations, fixed at the start of the game.
- There are other characters who can move and who will change the state of items.
- Locations can contain objects *(items)* that can be *taken* and *dropped* by some characters.
- There is a concept of time.

This description suggests the following entities:

- *You*, the entity that represents the central character
- *Location*, a place where a character can be
- Connection, connects locations
- *OtherCharacter*, characters in the game
- *Game*, a container for all things in the game
- *Item*, an object that can be taken or dropped
- *GameTime*, the time concept in the game

The next step is to find relationships among the entities found so far. The task is to identify those relationships; the details can be added later.

The following relationships were identified:

- An OtherCharacter will always be at one and only one location.
- An Item is either at a Location or held by a character.
- A Connection is a relation between two Locations.
- You and OtherCharacter appear have much behavior in common; therefore a parent entity, *GameCharacter,* was defined.

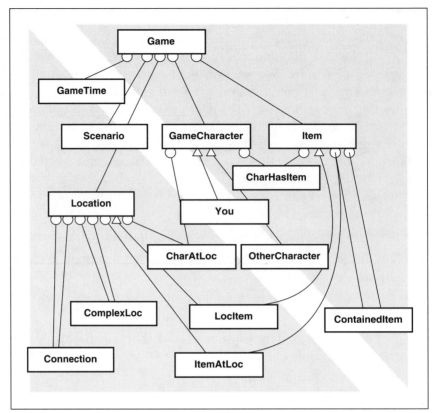

FIGURE B.1   Entity model of the Game application

Figure B.1 shows the entity model derived.

Entity: **ComplexLoc**
Describes a relation between Locations. In this way a maze can be described as consisting of several rooms or a large room as consisting of several corners.

Entity: **Connection**
Describes a relation between Locations. Connections are the paths along which a character can move from one room to another.

Entity: **ContainedItem**
Describes a membership relation between Items. An Item can be contained in another item, such as water in a bottle, or a cloak in a chest.

Entity: **Game**
There will be one instance of Game that will hold references to the instances, or if there are more, a set of instances of the associated entities.

Attributes:

log	Moves by the player and reaction by the game
status	The current status of the game

Actions:

restart	Resume a saved game.
load	Load a saved game.
save	Save a game.
start	Start a new game.
end	End a game.

Entity: **GameCharacter**

A character that can move through the maze. This entity will turn into a generic class, which should have no instances. It holds general properties that apply to all characters in the game.

Actions:

move	Move to a new location.
learn	Acknowledge that you have heard something.
hear	Hear something.
say	Say something.

Entity: **OtherCharacter**

OtherCharacters are those characters in the game that are not identified with the user.

Entity: **You**

The central character in the game. There will be only one instance of You.

Entity: **GameTime**

There will be an element of time in the game, although its use is not defined at this stage. Possibilities are

- Real time
- Clock ticks
- User interaction sequencing.

Entity: **Item**

This is the entity that generally describes the items in the game. Each particular type of Item, such as sword, book, or curtain, will probably have its own child entity to describe any specific properties it might have.

Attributes:

color
description
mass — The weight of the item
size — The size of the item

Actions:

printString	Return a character string describing the item.
pickUp	Move the association from the location where the item is, to the character who picks up the item.
listActions	Return a list of all actions that can be performed on the item.
location	The location where the item can be found.
drop	Move the association from the character that held the item to the location where the item is dropped.
throw	This should be implemented by subclasses in the object model. Initially it will be the same as *drop.*
location: aLocation	Put the item in the location specified by aLocation.

Entity: **LocItem**

This entity inherits properties from both Item and Location. It is used to describe items such as chests, where a character can be inside the chest, but if the character is strong enough, he or she can also hold the chest.

Entity: **Location**

Describes a location in the maze. Locations cannot be subdivided; therefore a character will always be at exactly one location.

Actions:

removeCharacter	Remove a character from the list of characters.
addCharacter: aCharacter	Add a character to the list of characters.
addItem: anItem	Add an item to the list of items.
removeItem: anItem	Remove an item from the list of items.

Entity: **Scenario**
There will be one instance of the Scenario class for each game. This entity will hold the *business rules* of the game.

Entity: **CharAtLoc**
Describes the relationship between the characters in the game and the location where they can be found.

Entity: **CharHasItem**
Contains instances that relate Item instances to specific GameCharacter instances. The existence of this entity stems from the modeling technique used by the analysis team. It will be implemented as an instance variable in both the Item and GameCharacter classes in the object model. The purpose of the relationship is to keep track of the items each character holds.

Entity: **ItemAtLoc**
Describes the relation between locations and items. It keeps track of what items are at a certain location.

Entity Tree Structure
GameCharacter—You
GameCharacter—OtherCharacter
Item—LocItem
Location—LocItem

Relationships
Game—Location
Game—Item
Game—GameTime
Game—Scenario
Game—GameCharacter
GameCharacter—CharAtLoc
GameCharacter—CharHasItem
Item—CharHasItem

Item—ItemAtLoc
Item—ContainedItem
Location—ComplexLoc
Location—ItemAtLoc
Location—Connection
Location—CharAtLoc
Location—ComplexLoc

B.4 Step 2: Application Scoping

The original model was considered too large for the initial implementation. Therefore, the decision was made to leave out entities that were not strictly necessary for producing a preliminary scenario: GameTime, Scenario, LocItem, and ContainedItem. This reduced the number of entities to ten.

B.5 Step 3: Transition to Object Modeling

The modeling notation used makes no clear distinction between entities and relationships or associations. Translating entities to classes usually requires some judgment and experience. In addition, in a class model some of the relations, depending on their complexity, may also be defined by classes.

Since the modeling was done at the real-world level (i.e., the entities were determined from user-identifiable objects), the mapping from entities to classes and from relationships to associations was straightforward. Therefore, the following classes were identified at this stage: You, Location, GameCharacter, OtherCharacter, Game, and Item.

A definition was required at this stage regarding whether the class You was different from the OtherCharacter class, and whether both classes could be combined into the superclass, GameCharacter. The decision was to model You as a separate class, because there was a sufficient semantic difference between the two classes.

There were also some special considerations with respect to the modeling of Connection, because it is defined as a relationship between Locations, and is therefore an association: its existence depends on the existence of the Locations. This association was implemented as a class, with *direction* as an attribute. The other associations in the game model are CharAtLoc, CharHasItem, and ItemAtLoc.

The associations were documented in a data dictionary indicating their structure. For example, CharAtLoc relates instances of Location and Character. For each Location, there can be more than one Character, but each Character can be at only one Location. Figure B.2 shows the class model obtained after Step 3.

B.6   Step 4: Model Transformations

Since this was the first iteration, and the model was comparatively simple, model transformations were not undertaken.

B.7   Step 5: Application model design

The starting point for the application design is the model shown in Figure B.2.

B.8   Step 6: User Interface: Interaction

The groundwork for structuring user tasks is done by specifying the business processes. A helpful way of refining a business process is to create a scenario for it, for example, "A Day in the Life of a User." The

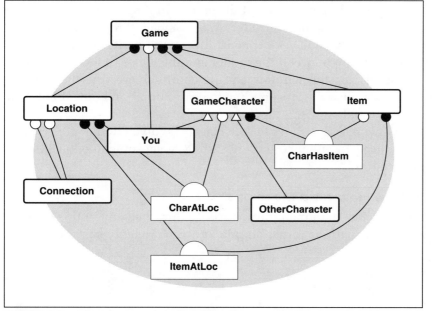

FIGURE B.2   The class model after Step 3.

scenario would involve a very specific example and should contain no conditional steps.

The First Scenario

The application development began with the following simple script, which represents the steps taken in a trivial version of the game (the tutorial aspects are ignored for the first iteration):

1. Begin game.

2. X is in a corridor.

3. X walks a certain distance along the corridor; there are doors to the right and left.

4. X opens a door on the left and looks in.

5. X sees a portion of the room and two items on the floor. One is a cloak and one a bottle.

6. X walks to the bottle and picks it up.

7. X picks up the cloak and puts it on.

8. X leaves the room.

Out of a simple scenario such as this could be constructed more significant scripts modeling an appropriate range of user tasks. The scenarios should be embodied in function that is present in the prototype and will be used during user testing and feedback. Scenarios also help to validate the model developed in Steps 1 to 4.

A new class, GameController, was designed. It represents the controller part of the model-view-controller structure. Its responsibility is to communicate between the model and the views (the onscreen representation, i.e., the window and its controls), creating them in the appropriate positions, responding to user actions, and refreshing their data as needed.

Sample message flows for the objects involved in the scenario can be produced to enhance understanding of the fundamental interactions required.

Message Flow for a Move of aYOU

The script can be refined into a message flow diagram. In this case the resulting scenario is rather simple. It can be roughly sketched as follows:

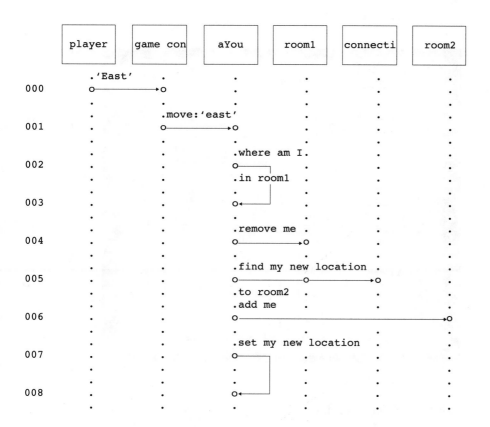

B.9 Step 7: User Interface: Representation

A first pass at the window layout was then attempted. This layout employed a single window for all user interaction. Pushbuttons allowed the user to move in four directions. A textual representation of the user character's location was displayed in a pane to the left. Items in the location were displayed in a listbox, as were items that the user was carrying. Pop-up menus were used to allow the user to manipulate these items (e.g., pick-up or drop, which would cause an item to be transferred from one listbox to another).

The user interface design was captured as shown in Figure B.3.

B.10 Step 8: Persistent Information Design

For the first iteration, the persistent information design was rather elementary. It consists of a flat file with a simple syntax for organizing the entries, in which can be stored definitions of Locations, Characters,

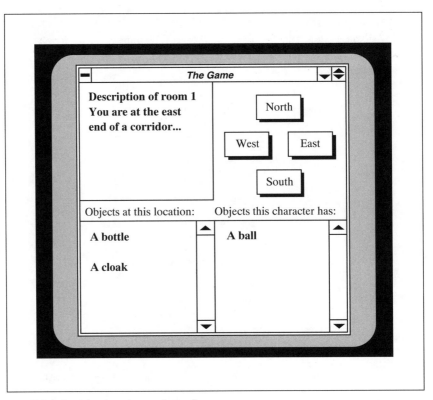

FIGURE B.3   Version 1 user interface

Items, and Connections. The file is supported for input to the game only.

B.11 Step 9: Implementation

The final design diagram of the first iteration is shown in Figure B.4.

The Smalltalk code implementing this design is shown in Appendix C, "Smalltalk Code of the First Iteration." The model classes were implemented as specified.

B.12 Step 10: User Feedback

User feedback was elicited through a series of unstructured demonstrations leading up to a more formal usability review. The former ensure that the users are familiar with the general implementation of the model, and the latter aims to test in detail whether the user interface is sufficiently effective and intuitive for the tasks the user has to perform.

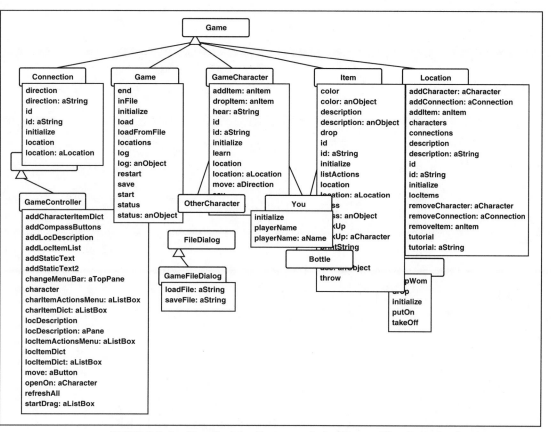

FIGURE B.4   The design diagram of the Game (first iteration)

It became clear that the Game interface needed to be far more subtle and complex, and that it should be driven through images rather than textual representations.

B.13 Step 11: Iteration

The simple implementation of the first iteration can now be enhanced by returning to Step 4 and the subsequent modeling and design. More of the full set of requirements can be represented in the object model, user interface design, and code implementation. The behavior of Item and the variety of its subclasses needed to be enhanced, goals had to be added for the GameCharacter, the relationship between Item and Connection had to be enriched so as to support dependencies between them, and so on.

In addition, during the first iteration, new ideas occurred that influenced the subsequent development of the application and had to be incorporated in the same way.

Appendix C

Smalltalk Code of the First Iteration

This appendix gives the full Smalltalk/V PM source code produced during the first iteration of the development process.

The game is instantiated by sending the following messages:

Game new initialize loadFromFile

This causes the standard OS/2 file dialog to appear. From the list of files, it is necessary to chose a maze file. This file contains a set of instructions describing the structure of a maze and the elements found within it. An example of a maze file is shown below:

```
loc@0@a yellow room@tutorial for the yellow room@
loc@1@a green corridor@tutorial for the green corridor@
loc@2@the purple library@tutorial for the purple library@
con@10@0@north@1@
con@11@1@south@0@
con@12@1@west@2@
con@13@2@east@1@
itm@20@Cloak@a red cloak@0@
itm@21@Cloak@a blue cloak@0@
itm@22@Bottle@a transparent bottle@2@
you@0@
```

The file shows three locations with connections between them and items in them. The first field identifies the type of record, i.e., Item, Connection, Character, or Location and the second provides a key. The other fields are specific to the record type.

The third field of a location record contains a description, the fourth a tutorial string. The third and fifth fields of a connection record contain the locations that are being connected, and the fourth contains a direction. The third field of an item record contains the item class name, the fourth a description, and the fifth its location.

Fields are delimited by a single character. Records can appear in any order within the file, and there is no limit to their number.

C.1 Class Definitions

Class Connection

```
Object subclass: #Connection
   instanceVariableNames:
      ' direction id location '
   classVariableNames: ''
   poolDictionaries: ''
```

Instance methods of class Connection

```
direction
   "get the direction of this connection"


   ^direction.

direction: aString
   "set the direction of this connection"


   direction := aString.

id


   ^id

id: aString


   id := aString.

initialize
   "** not implemented in this iteration **"

location
   "return the location this connection connects to"


   ^location

location: aLocation
   "set the target location of this connection"


   location := aLocation.
```

Class Game

```
Object subclass: #Game
  instanceVariableNames:
    ' rLocation rScenario rItem status log rGameCharacter
      rGameTime you rConnection '
  classVariableNames: ' '
  poolDictionaries:
    ' CharacterConstants '
```

Instance methods of class Game

```
end
    "End a game"
  "** not implemented in this iteration **"


inFile
    "Find the input filename"
  | fileName file dialog |

    dialog := GameFileDialog new loadFile.
    fileName := dialog file.
      fileName isNil ifTrue: [^nil].
    file := File pathName: fileName.
    ^file.


initialize
    " initialize the instance variables that hold references to the model
      classes "

    rLocation := Dictionary new.
    rItem := Dictionary new.
    rGameCharacter := Dictionary new.
    rConnection := Dictionary new.


load
    "Load a saved game"
  "** not implemented in this iteration **"


loadFromFile
    "this method will ask for a game file to be loaded
     and set up the game"
  | stream entry fieldDelimiter game type field1 field2 |
```

```
        self initialize.
        stream := self inFile.
        fieldDelimiter := $@.


        [stream atEnd] whileFalse:
          [
          type := stream upTo: fieldDelimiter.

          ( type = 'con' ) ifTrue:
             [ entry := Connection new initialize.
               entry id: ( stream upTo: fieldDelimiter ).
               field1 := ( stream upTo: fieldDelimiter ).
               entry direction: ( stream upTo: fieldDelimiter ).
               entry location: ( rLocation at: ( stream upTo: fieldDelimiter )).
               ( rLocation at: field1 ) addConnection: entry.
               rConnection at: (entry id copy) put: (entry copy).
               stream upTo: Lf
             ].

         ( type = 'itm' ) ifTrue:
           [ field1 := stream upTo: fieldDelimiter.
             field2 := stream upTo: fieldDelimiter.
             ( field2 = 'Bottle' )
               ifTrue: [ entry := Bottle new initialize]
               ifFalse: [
                    ( field2 = 'Cloak' )
                  ifTrue: [ entry := Cloak new initialize]
                  ifFalse: [ entry := Item new initialize]
                         ].
             entry id: field1.
             entry description: ( stream upTo: fieldDelimiter ).
             entry location: ( rLocation at: (stream upTo: fieldDelimiter )).
             rItem at: (entry id copy) put: (entry copy).
             entry location addItem: entry.
             stream upTo: Lf
             ].

          ( type = 'you' ) ifTrue:
             [ you := You new initialize.
               you id: 'you'.
               you location: ( rLocation at: (stream upTo: fieldDelimiter )).
               you location addCharacter: you.
               stream upTo: Lf
             ].
```

```
      ( type = 'loc' ) ifTrue:
        [ entry := Location new initialize.
          entry id: ( stream upTo: fieldDelimiter ).
          entry description: ( stream upTo: fieldDelimiter ).
          entry tutorial: ( stream upTo: fieldDelimiter ).
          rLocation at: (entry id copy) put: (entry copy).
          stream upTo: Lf
        ].
  ].

  stream close.

  GameController new openOn: you.

locations
    " answer the reference to the set of locations "
  ^ rLocation.

log

  ^log

log: anObject

  log := anObject

start
    "Start a new game"
  "** not implemented in this iteration **"

status

  ^status

status: anObject

  status := anObject
```

Class GameCharacter

```
Object subclass: #GameCharacter
  instanceVariableNames:
    ' rCharAtLoc aSaidString id rCharHasItem '
  classVariableNames: ''
  poolDictionaries: ''
```

Instance methods of class GameCharacter

```
addItem: anItem
    " add an item to the set of items "


    rCharHasItem at: (anItem id) put: anItem.


dictOfItems
    " return the dictionary of items this character has "


    ^ rCharHasItem.


dropItem: anItem
    " remove an item from the set of items "


    rCharHasItem removeKey: (anItem id) ifAbsent: [].


hear: aString
    " Hear and remember comments from other parts of the model. "


    aSaidString := aString.


id


    ^.id


id: aString


    id := aString


initialize
    " initialize some things for a character "


    ^ rCharHasItem := Dictionary new.


learn
    "** not implemented in this iteration **"
```

```
location
    "Return the location where the character can be found. "


    ^rCharAtLoc.

location: aLocation
    " Set the location where the character can be found. "

    rCharAtLoc := aLocation.

move: aDirection
    " Put the character into a location "
    | loc con newloc |

    loc := self location.
    con := loc connections at: aDirection ifAbsent: [&caret.nil].
    loc removeCharacter: self.
    newloc := con location.
    newloc addCharacter: self.
    self location: newloc.

say
    " Repeat back anything that has been heard -
    then forget it. "
    | aString |

    aString := aSaidString.
    aSaidString := nil.
    ^aString.
```

Class OtherCharacter

```
GameCharacter subclass: #OtherCharacter
    instanceVariableNames: ''
    classVariableNames: ''
    poolDictionaries: ''
```

Instance methods of class OtherCharacter

```
"** not implemented in this iteration **"
```

Class You

```
GameCharacter subclass: #You
    instanceVariableNames:
```

```
        ' playerName '
    classVariableNames: ''
    poolDictionaries: ''
```

Instance methods of class You

```
initialize
    " Initialize the name of the player. "

    super initialize.
    playerName := 'You'.


playerName
    " Return a name for the instance You"


    ^playerName


playerName: aString
    " Permit the name of the player to be recorded. "


    playerName := aString.
```

Class Item

```
Object subclass: #Item
    instanceVariableNames:
        ' rItemAtLoc  size  rCharHasItem  id  rContainedItem  description
          mass color '
    classVariableNames: ''
    poolDictionaries: ''
```

Instance methods of class Item

```
color
    " get an item's color "


    ^color


color: anObject
    " set an item's color "


    color := anObject.


description
    " return an item's description "
```

```
    ^description

description: anObject
    " set an item's description "

    description := anObject.

drop
    " Move the association from the character that held the item to the
    location where the item is dropped. "

    " The item must be held for the character to be able to drop it. "
    (rCharHasItem = nil)
        ifTrue: [^nil].

    "Ask the character where it is and put the item there. "
    rItemAtLoc := rCharHasItem location.
    rItemAtLoc addItem: self.
    rCharHasItem dropItem: self.
    rCharHasItem := nil.

id
    " get an item's id "

    ^id

id: aString
    " set an item's id "

    id := aString.

initialize
    " initialize some things for items "

    description := 'an undefined item'.
    rContainedItem := Set new.
    mass := 0.
    size := 0.

listActions
    " Return a list of all actions that can be performed on an item.
    The actions depend on whether the item is held or not. "
```

```
| dict |
dict := Dictionary new.
(rItemAtLoc = nil)
  ifFalse: [ dict at: 'pick up' put: #pickUp]
  ifTrue: [
     dict at: 'drop' put: #drop.
     dict at: 'throw' put: #throw
           ].
dict at: 'describe' put: #description.
^dict
```

```
location
    " Get the location of an item "


  ^ItemAtLoc
```

```
location: aLocation
    " Put the item at a location "


  rItemAtLoc:= aLocation.
```

```
mass
    " get an item's mass "


  ^mass.
```

```
mass: anObject
    " set an item's mass "


  mass := anObject.
```

```
pickUp
    " find the You character that is picking item up "


  self pickUp: (self location characters at: 'you').
```

```
pickUp: aCharacter
    " Move the association from the location where the item is,
    to the character that picked up the item. "


  rCharHasItem := aCharacter.
  aCharacter addItem: self.
  rItemAtLoc removeItem: self.
```

```
        rItemAtLoc := nil.
    printString
        " Return a character string describing the item. "

        ^self class name.

    size
        " get an item's size "

        ^size

    size: anObject
        " set an item's size "

        size := anObject.

    throw
        " This should be implemented by subclasses.
        Initially set to the same as drop. "

        self drop.
```

Class Bottle

```
    Item subclass: #Bottle
        instanceVariableNames: ''
        classVariableNames: ''
        poolDictionaries: ''
```

Instance methods of class Bottle

```
        "** not implemented in this iteration **"
```

Class Cloak

```
    Item subclass: #Cloak
        instanceVariableNames:
          ' cloakWorn '
        classVariableNames: ''
        poolDictionaries: ''
```

Instance methods of class Cloak

```
    cloakWorn
        " Get the status of the cloak - is it being worn or not? "

        ^cloakWorn
```

```
drop
    "The cloak cannot be dropped if it is being worn by a character. "

 (cloakWorn)
   ifTrue: [You hear: 'How can you drop something you are wearing?']
   ifFalse: [super drop].


initialize
    " Initialize a cloak "

 super initialize.
 cloakWorn := false.


putOn
    " the cloak must be worn, rather than just carried, to feel
    its benefits. "

 (rCharHasItem = nil)
   ifFalse: [
      cloakWorn := true.
      You hear: 'That is a lot warmer.'
            ]
   ifTrue: [You hear: 'You do not have a cloak to put on.'&r
brk..


takeOff
    " the cloak must be taken off before it can be dropped "

 (cloakWorn)
   ifTrue: [cloakWorn := false]
   ifFalse: [You hear: 'You are not wearing a cloak.'].
```

Class Location

```
Object subclass: #Location
  instanceVariableNames:
    ' description rItemAtLoc tutorial rConnection id rCharAtLoc '
  classVariableNames: ''
  poolDictionaries: ''
```

Instance methods of class Location

```
addCharacter: aCharacter
    " Add a character to the dictionary of characters at this location. "
```

```
rCharAtLoc at: (aCharacter id) put: aCharacter.

addConnection: aConnection
    " Add a connection to the dictionary of connections at this location. "

    rConnection at: (aConnection direction) put: aConnection.

addItem: anItem
    " Add an item to the dictionary of items at this location. "

    rItemAtLoc at: (anItem id) put: anItem.

characters
    " get the dictionary of characters "

    ^rCharAtLoc

connections
    " get the dictionary of connections from this location "

    ^rConnection.

description
    " get a location's description "

    ^description .

description: anObject
    " set a location's description "

    description := anObject.

id
    " get an item's id "

    ^id

id: aString
    " set an item's id "

    id := aString.

initialize
```

```
        " initialize references to associated model objects "
    description := 'an undefined location'.
    rConnection := Dictionary new.
    rCharAtLoc := Dictionary new.
    rItemAtLoc := Dictionary new.


locItems
    " get the dictionary of items in this location "


    ^rItemAtLoc


removeCharacter: aCharacter
    " remove a character from the dictionary of characters
    in this location "


    ^rCharAtLoc removeKey: (aCharacter id) ifAbsent: [&rbrk..


removeConnection: aConnection
    " Remove a connection from the dictionary of connections
    at this location. "


    rConnection removeKey: (aConnection id) ifAbsent: [].


removeItem: anItem
    " remove an item from the dictionary of items in this location "


    ^rItemAtLoc removeKey: (anItem id) ifAbsent: [].


tutorial
    " get the tutorial information "


    ^tutorial


tutorial: aString
    " Set the tutorial information "


    tutorial := aString
```

Class CameController

```
ViewManager subclass: #GameController
    instanceVariableNames:
        ' character locDescription locItemDict charItemDict '
    classVariableNames: ''
```

```
        poolDictionaries: ''
```

Instance methods of class GameController

```
addCharacterItemList
    " display list of character's items in right bottom quadrant "

    self addSubpane:
      ( ListBox new
        owner: self;
        when: #getContents perform: #charItemDict:;
        when: #getMenu perform: #charItemActionsMenu:;
        when: #doubleClickSelect perform: #charItemActionsMenu&colon.;
        framingRatio:
          ( ( Rectangle leftBottomUnit right: (1/2) )
            extentFromLeftBottom: ( (1/2) @ (1/3) ) )
      ).


addCompassButtons
    " display North, South, East, West as buttons "

    self addSubpane:
      ( Button new
        owner: self;
        contents: 'North';
        when: #clicked perform: #move:;
        framingRatio:
          ( ( ( Rectangle leftTopUnit down: (1/20) ) right: (13/20
) )
            extentFromLeftTop: ( (1/6) @ (2/20 ) ) )
      ).
    self addSubpane:
      ( Button new
        owner: self;
        contents: 'South';
        when: #clicked perform: #move:;
        framingRatio:
          ( ( ( Rectangle leftTopUnit down: (6/20) ) right: (13/20
) )
            extentFromLeftTop: ( (1/6) @ (2/20 ) ) )
      ).
    self addSubpane:
      ( Button new
```

```
            owner: self;
            contents: 'West';
            when: #clicked perform: #move:;
            framingRatio:
              ( ( ( Rectangle leftTopUnit down: (7/40) ) right: (11/20
  ) )
              extentFromLeftTop: ( (1/6) @ (2/20 ) ) )
        ).
      self addSubpane:
        ( Button new
          owner: self;
          contents: 'East';
          when: #clicked perform: #move:;
          framingRatio:
            ( ( ( Rectangle leftTopUnit down: (7/40) ) right: (15/20
  ) )
            extentFromLeftTop: ( (1/6) @ (2/20 ) ) )
        ).


addLocDescription
      " display room description in left top quadrant "

    self addSubpane:
      ( TextPane new
        owner: self;
        when: #getContents perform: #locDescription:;
        framingRatio:
          ( Rectangle leftTopUnit extentFromLeftTop: ( (1/2) @ (1/2) ) )
      ;
              enableWordWrap
      ).


addLocItemList
      " display list of items in room in left bottom quadrant "

    self addSubpane:
      ( ListBox new
        owner: self;
        when: #getContents perform: #locItemDict:;
        when: #getMenu perform: #locItemActionsMenu:;
        when: #getPopupMenu perform: #locItemActionsMenu:;
        framingRatio:
```

```
            ( Rectangle leftBottomUnit extentFromLeftBottom: ( (1/2) @ (1/ 3) ) ) )
        ).
addStaticText
    " text describing what will appear in left bottom quadrant "

    self addSubpane:
      ( StaticText new
        owner: self;
        leftJustified;
        contents: 'The objects in this location:';
        framingRatio:
          ( ( Rectangle leftTopUnit down: (11/20) )
            extentFromLeftTop: ( (1/2) @ (2/20 ) ) ) )
      ).


addStaticText2
    " text describing what will appear in right bottom quadrant "

    self addSubpane:
      ( StaticText new
        owner: self;
        leftJustified;
        contents: 'The objects held by you:';
        framingRatio:
          ((( Rectangle leftTopUnit down: (11/20) ) right: (1/2) )
            extentFromLeftTop: ( (1/2) @ (2/20 ) ) ) )
      ).


changeMenuBar: aTopPane
    " remove standard Smalltalk menus "

    aTopPane menuWindow
      removeMenu: ( aTopPane menuWindow menuTitled: 'File' );
      removeMenu: ( aTopPane menuWindow menuTitled: 'Edit' );
      removeMenu: ( aTopPane menuWindow menuTitled: 'Smalltalk' ).


character
    " return character "

    ^character


charItemActionsMenu: aListBox
```

```
        " put up menu of actions for character's items listbox "
        | anItem aDictionary aMenu selected |
        anItem := charItemDict at: (aListBox selectedItem)
        ifAbsent: [].
        (anItem isNil)
          ifFalse: [
             aDictionary := anItem listActions.
             aMenu := Menu new title: 'CharItemActions'.
             aMenu owner: anItem.
             aDictionary keys do:
               [:i | aMenu appendItem: i selector: (aDictionary at: i)].
             selected := aMenu popUp.
             (selected isNil)
               ifFalse: [anItem perform: selected.
                          self refreshAll ]
             ].


charItemDict: aListBox
     " display list box items from charItemDict "

  aListBox contents: charItemDict keys asOrderedCollection.


locDescription
     " return contents of location description "

  ^locDescription


locDescription: aPane
     " display list box items from locItemList "

  aPane contents: self locDescription


locItemActionsMenu: aListBox
     " put up test menu for location listbox "
     | anItem aDictionary aMenu selected |

  anItem := locItemDict at: ( aListBox selectedItem ) ifAbsent:. [].
  (anItem isNil)
     ifFalse: [
        aDictionary := anItem listActions.
        aMenu := Menu new title: 'LocItemActions'.
        aMenu owner: anItem.
```

```
        aDictionary keys do:
          [:i | aMenu appendItem: i selector: (aDictionary at: i)].
        selected := aMenu popUp.
        (selected isNil)
          ifFalse: [anItem perform: selected.
                        self refreshAll ]
            ].


locItemDict
    " return contents of location ItemList "


   ^locItemDict


locItemDict: aListBox
    " display list box items from locItemDict "


   aListBox contents: locItemDict keys asOrderedCollection.


move: aButton
    " respond to compass buttons "


   (aButton contents = 'East')
     ifTrue: [character move: 'east'].
   (aButton contents = 'West')
     ifTrue: [character move: 'west'].
   (aButton contents = 'North')
     ifTrue: [character move: 'north'].
   (aButton contents = 'South')
     ifTrue: [character move: 'south'].
   self refreshAll.


noMenu: aPane
    " do not display menu "


openOn: aCharacter
    " create a game window consisting of 4 quadrants "


   character := aCharacter.
   self label: 'The game';
        addLocDescription;
        addLocItemList;
        addStaticText;
```

```
            addStaticText2;
            addCompassButtons;
            addCharacterItemList;
            refreshAll.
    self when: #menuBuilt perform: #changeMenuBar:.
    self openWindow.


refreshAll
    " Update location description from location
    where character is and locItemList similarly.

    Update charItemDict from the character's setOfItems,
    getting in addition the description for each item. "
    | aLocItemDictByID aCharItemDictByID |


locDescription := character location description.
aLocItemDictByID := character location locItems.
locItemDict := Dictionary new.
aLocItemDictByID do:
    [:i | locItemDict at: (i description)
    put: i].
aCharItemDictByID := character dictOfItems.
charItemDict := Dictionary new.
aCharItemDictByID do:
    [:i | charItemDict at: (i description)
    put: i].
self changed: #locItemDict:;
    changed: #locDescription:;
    changed: #charItemDict:.
```

Bibliography

[AIK92]   Jan Aikins. "CASE, KBS and Object–Oriented
            Programming." Tutorial at AAAI–92, California.

[BEC89]   Kent Beck and Ward Cunningham. "A Laboratory for
            Teaching Object-Oriented Thinking. OOPSLA 1989
            Proceedings, pp.1–6.

[BOO92]   Grady Booch. *Object Oriented Analysis and Design
            with Applications.* Benjamin/Cummings.

[BRO87]   Fred Brooks. *No Silver Bullet.* IEEE Computer (April
            1987).

[BOW91]   Adrian J. Bowles. "Perspective: Investing in Objects
            Today." *Hotline on Object-Oriented Technology,*
            Volume 2, Number 12 (October).

[BUL91]   David Bulman. "A Modest Survey of OOD
            Approaches." *Hotline on Object-Oriented Technology,*
            Volume 2, Number 12 (October).

[CAT91]   R. G. G. Cattell. *Object Data Management.* Addison-
            Wesley.

[CHA92]   Dennis D'Champeaux and Penelope Faure. "A
            Comparative Study of Object-Oriented Analysis
            Methods." *Journal of Object-Oriented Programming,*
            Volume 5, Number 1 (March).

[COA91a]   Peter Coad and Edward Yourdon. *Object-Oriented
            Analysis.* Prentice-Hall.

[COA91b]   Peter Coad and Edward Yourdon. *Object-Oriented
            Design.* Prentice Hall.

[COK93] Dick Conklin. "OS/2 Developer." *Spotlite on Digitalk* (September/October 1993).

[CON92] Michael Connell. "Adopting Objects: Pitfalls." *Hotline on Object-Oriented Technology*, Volume 3, Number 3 (January).

[COX90] Brad Cox. *Object-Oriented Programming, An Evolutionary Approach.* Addison-Wesley, 1986.

[DEN91a] Richard J. DeNatale and Rodney A. Smith. *Technologies for Supporting Frameworks: An Example.* IBM Technical Report, TR 29.1279 (November).

[DEN91b] Richard J. DeNatale and Rodney A. Smith. *Frameworks: A Fresh Look at Software Reuse.* IBM Technical Report, TR-29.1280 (November 1991).

[DIE89] Dietrich Walter et al. "Saving a Legacy with Objects." OOPSLA 1989 *Proceedings,* pp. 77–83.

[DOB89] *Dr. Dobb's Journal,* Number 158 (December).

[DUN92] Jeff Duntemann. "Vujá Dé," *Dr. Dobb's Journal* (March) 1992.

[FOW91] Martin Fowler. "Which OO Analysis and Design Method?" SCOOP Europe, September 1991.

[GAS89] Chris Gane and Trish Sarson. *Structured Systems Analysis: Tools and Techniques,* Prentice-Hall 1979.

[GEE89] C. S. Gee. *A Methodology for Object-Oriented Design.* IBM International Technical Support Center, Roanoke, Texas.

[GIB90] Elisabeth Gibson. "Objects—Born and Bred." *Byte* (October).

[GOL89] Adele Goldberg and David Robson. *Smalltalk 80: The Language.* Addison-Wesley.

[GOL92]   Adele Goldberg and Kenneth Rubin. "Object-Oriented Project Management." OOPSLA 1992, Tutorial.

[GUT91]   Michael Guttman and Jason Matthews. "The Object Mangement Group—A Window of Opportunity for Everyone." *Hotline on Object-Oriented Technology*, Volume 2, Number 12 (October).

[HAR89]   William H. Harrison, John J. Shilling, and Peter F. Sweeney. "Good News, Bed News: Experience Building a Software Development Environment Using the Object-Oriented Paradigm." OOPSLA 1989, *Proceedings*. Addison-Wesley.

[HEL90]   Richard Helm et al. "Contracts: Specifying Behavioral Compositions in Object-Oriented Systems." ECOOP/OOPSLA 1990 *Proceedings*.

[HEL93]   Richard Helm et al. *Design Patterns: Abstraction and Reuse of Object-Oriented Design.* IBM Technical Report, RC-18847, 1993.

[HEN90]   Brian Henderson-Sellers and Julian M. Edwards. "The Object-Oriented Systems Life Cycle." *Communications of the ACM*, Volume 33, Number 9 (September).

[HEN92a]   Brian Henderson-Sellers. "Adoption Rate of Object Technology: A Survey of NSW Industry." *Hotline on Object-Oriented Technology*, Volume 3, Number 3 (January).

[HEN92b]   Brian Henderson-Sellers. *A Book of Object-Oriented Knowledge.* Prentice-Hall.

[JAC92]   Ivar Jacobson. *Object Oriented Software Engineering.* Addison-Wesley, 1992.

[LEN91]   Marie A. Lenzi. "Object Statistics on the Way." *Hotline on Object-Oriented Technology*, Volume 2, Number 11 (September).

[LOO92]   Mary E. S. Loomis. "Object Database-Integrator for PCTE." *Journal of Object-Oriented Programming*, Volume 5, Number 2 (May).

[LOR91]   Mark Lorenz. *Object-Oriented Development: Team Roles and Perspectives*. IBM Technical Report, TR 29.1236 (September).

[LOR93]   Mark Lorenz. *A Process and Methodology for Devloping Object-Oriented Software Systems—A Practical Guide.* Prentice-Hall, 1993.

[LOV92]   Tom Love. *Hotline on Object-Oriented Technology*, Volume 3, Number 4 (February).

[LUK92]   Paul Luker. *Seminar on Object-Oriented Analysis and Design.* California State University at Chico.

[MEY88]   Bertrand Meyer. *Object-Oriented Software Construction.* Prentice-Hall.

[MON91]   Stephen Montgomery. *AD/Cycle.* Van Nostrand Reinhold.

[NOR91]   Donald Norman. *The Design of Everyday Things.* Basic Books.

[OMG90]   Object Management Group. *Object Management Architecture Guide.* OMG TC Document 90.9.1 (November).

[ONA91]   Adnan Adam Onart. "On Objects and Bullets." *Hotline on Object-Oriented Technology*, Volume 2, Number 11 (September).

[OOP91]   OOPSLA 1991 Report. "Designing Reusable Designs: Experiences Designing Object-Oriented Frameworks." OOPSLA/ECOOP 1991 Addendum to the *Proceedings* (Ottawa, Canada).

[POL92]   Paul Pollard et al. *Building Client/Server Applications with CICS and a GUI.* GG24-3855, IBM.

[RUM91]   James Rumbaugh et al. *Object-Oriented Modeling and Design*. Prentice-Hall.

[RYM93]   John Rymer. "IBM's System Object Model." *Distributed Computing Monitor*, Volume 8, Number 3 (March).

[SHE92]   Robert Shelton. "Enterprise Object Modeling: Knowing What We Know." *Hotline on Object-Oriented Technology*, Volume 3, Number 3 (January).

[SHL88]   S. Shlaer and S. J. Mellor. *Object-Oriented Systems Analysis*. Yourdon Press.

[SHL91]   S. Shlaer and S. J. Mellor. *Object Life Cycles: Modeling the World in States*. Yourdon Press.

[SHU88]   Nan C. Shu. *Visual Programming*. Van Nostrand Reinhold.

[SIM98]   Oliver Sims. *New World Object-Oriented Programming Concepts*. IBM UK Technical Support, United Kingdom.

[SMI91]   David N. Smith. *Concepts of Object-Oriented Programming*. McGraw-Hill.

[SMI92]   Larry Smith. *Software Reuse in Japan*. Software Technology Support Center, Ogden ALC/TISAC.

[TAY91]   David A. Taylor. *Object-Oriented Technology: A Manager's Guide*. Servio Corporation.

[TAY92]   David A. Taylor. *Object-Oriented Information Systems: Planning and Implementation*. John Wiley & Sons, Inc.

[TKA91]   Daniel Tkach et al. *Client/Server Computing: Application Design Guidelines*. GG24-3727, IBM.

[TKA93]   Daniel Tkach. "Strategies for Object-Oriented Technology Transfer." Position Paper, ACM SIGPLAN OOPSLA '93 Conference *Proceedings*, Washington, DC, 1993.

[ULL88]   Jeffrey D. Ullman. *Principles of Database and Knowledge-Base Systems.* Volume 1. Computer Science Press.

[URL91]   Zack Urlocker. "From Applications to Frameworks." *Hotline on Object-Oriented Technology*, Volume 2, Number 11 (September).

[VIN92]   Jim Vincent et al. *Introducing Object Technology in AD/Cycle.* IBM Technical Report TR29.1337.

[WAS91]   Anthony I. Wasserman. "The Spiral Model for Object Software Development." *Hotline on Object-Oriented Technology*, Volume 2, Number 3 (January).

[WAS92]   Anthony I. Wasserman. "Behavior and Scenarios for Object-Oriented Development." *Journal of Object-Oriented Programming* (February).

[WEG89]   Peter Wegner. *Concepts and Paradigms of Object-Oriented Programming.* OOPSLA 1989 *Proceedings.*

[WIR89]   Rebecca Wirfs-Brock and Brian Wilkerson. *Object-Oriented Design: A Responsibility-Driven Approach.* OOPSLA 1989 *Proceedings.*

[WIR90]   Rebecca Wirfs-Brock et al. *Designing Object-Oriented Software.* Prentice-Hall.

[WIR92]   Rebecca Wirfs-Brock. *Object Design.* IBM SREC Lecture Series, August 1992.

[YOU91]   Edward Yourdon. *Object-Oriented Analysis and Design.* Handout at the International IBM Academy Seminar, the Hague, 22–23 April.

[YOU92]   Edward Yourdon. *Decline and Fall of the American Programmer.* Yourdon Press (Prentice-Hall).

[ZDO89]   Stanley B. Zdonik and David Maier, eds. *Readings in Object-Oriented Database systems.* Morgan Kaufman Publishers.

Index